Randolph Ll Hodgson

Wanderings through unknown Austria

Randolph Ll Hodgson

Wanderings through unknown Austria

ISBN/EAN: 9783337198015

Printed in Europe, USA, Canada, Australia, Japan

Cover: Foto ©Andreas Hilbeck / pixelio.de

More available books at **www.hansebooks.com**

TRAVELS IN UNKNOWN AUSTRIA

MARY THURN-TAXIS

WANDERINGS

THROUGH

UNKNOWN AUSTRIA

BY

RANDOLPH LL. HODGSON

WITH ILLUSTRATIONS BY

MARY, PRINCESS OF THURN AND TAXIS

London
MACMILLAN AND CO., Limited
NEW YORK: THE MACMILLAN COMPANY
1896

CONTENTS

	PAGE
INTRODUCTION	1

CHAPTER I
Duino   7

CHAPTER II
Duino—*continued*   17

CHAPTER III
Miramar   29

CHAPTER IV
The Timavo and San Giovanni   39

CHAPTER V
A Rainy Day   51

CHAPTER VI

Aquileia . . 62

CHAPTER VII

Villa Vicentina 76

CHAPTER VIII

Sagrado and Gradisca . . 85

CHAPTER IX

On Ghosts 96

CHAPTER X

Capodistria . . . 108

CHAPTER XI

Goritz . . 121

CHAPTER XII

On Nothing at all 132

CONCLUSION 141

ILLUSTRATIONS

	PAGE
MARY THURN-TAXIS .	*Frontispiece*
HEADPIECE TO INTRODUCTION	1
TAILPIECE TO INTRODUCTION	5
CASTLE DUINO . . .	6
HEADPIECE TO CHAPTER I.	7
DUINO FROM THE SEA	8
DOOR-KNOCKER	10
BOREAS .	12
THE ROMAN TOWER .	14
TAILPIECE TO CHAPTER I.	16
THE BALCONY . . .	18
PORTRAIT OF MATTHEW HOFER (Van Dyck)	21
THE BANQUETING HALL .	22
THE RIVIERA .	25
A RECESS IN THE LIBRARY	26
TAILPIECE TO CHAPTER II.	28
INITIAL LETTER TO CHAPTER III.	29
MIRAMAR	32
THE RISING MOON	36

	PAGE
TAILPIECE TO CHAPTER III.	38
INITIAL LETTER TO CHAPTER IV.	39
SPRINGS OF THE TIMAVO	41
CASTLE DUINO FROM THE ROMAN ROAD	48
TAILPIECE TO CHAPTER IV.	50
INITIAL LETTER TO CHAPTER V.	51
THE GROTTO ROOM	53
CASTLE DUINO FROM THE MOAT	57
THE RUIN	59
TAILPIECE TO CHAPTER V.	61
INITIAL LETTER TO CHAPTER VI.	62
FISHING BOAT (BRAGOZZO)	66
GRADO—THE HARBOUR	67
THE CHURCH AT GRADO	68
ENTRANCE TO CASTLE DUINO	74
TAILPIECE TO CHAPTER VI.	75
INITIAL LETTER TO CHAPTER VII.	76
LITTLE RIVER NEAR VILLA VICENTINA	78
VILLA VICENTINA	79
TAILPIECE TO CHAPTER VII.	84
INITIAL LETTER TO CHAPTER VIII.	85
PALAZZO FINETTI	90
HOUSE AT GRADISCA	91
TOMB OF NICOLAO DELLA TORRE	92
TAILPIECE TO CHAPTER VIII.	95
INITIAL LETTER TO CHAPTER IX.	96
THE WHITE LADY	98

Illustrations

	PAGE
The White Lady	99
Tin-ho—First-class Mandarin	101
Tailpiece to Chapter IX.	107
Initial Letter to Chapter X.	108
The Town Hall	115
Door-knocker	118
Café at Capodistria	119
Initial Letter to Chapter XI.	121
A Cast	125
Girl from Duino	129
Castle Duino from the Railway	130
Tailpiece to Chapter XI.	131
Initial Letter to Chapter XII.	132
Lawn-tennis Ground	138
Entrance to the Village of Duino	139
Initial Letter to Conclusion	141
Tailpiece to Conclusion	143

INTRODUCTION

Here where the world is quiet.
                               SWINBURNE.

WE were talking the other day of the many and interesting books of travel that have been written lately, books so full of valuable information and precise descriptions that you almost feel that Inner

Africa and the North Pole are as familiar to you as Piccadilly and Oxford Street.

"It is a blessing that such books exist," said our host, who has rather a philosophical turn of mind. "Of course, I never read them; personally, I think that reading and writing are decidedly a mistake; but if I *wanted* to know anything about these countries there would not be the slightest necessity to travel about; other people have done that for me. To speak the truth, I do *not* want to know anything about foreign parts. One book of Stanley, for instance, is enough to make me hate the very idea of Inner Africa; and as to the North Pole, I cannot describe my feelings with regard to the raving lunatics who imagine they have anything to do there. I am all for a quiet life, you know. I stick to my principles—the summer in Cairo, the winter in bed."

This speech was received with icy coldness. We are not philosophically inclined, I am sorry to say, and though I should not much like Inner Africa on account of the heat, I have always cherished the idea of some day making a trip to the North Pole.

This I said with my usual diffidence and modesty, but of course I was hooted by the rest of the company, and one energetic lady explained at great length that the North Pole is a "humbug." Another lady (the one who is my collaborator now) confessed a great partiality for travelling. "Only," she said, "it is not at all necessary to go so far; there are many wonderful countries in Europe which are very little known. For instance," she added, turning to me, "I always wonder how very little you English know of Austria. The fact that Vienna is a pretty town, where everything English is particularly liked; that Prague is a fine old city, and that here and there we have first-rate shooting, is about all that is known of Austria by foreigners. And it is a pity! Who really has seen the wonderful mountains of the Tyrol, mountains that are just as fine as any in Switzerland; the charming lakes of the Salzkammergut; the green valleys of that greenest of lands, Styria? Who has spoken of the mysterious charm of the great Bohemian forests of oak and pine, the quaint little towns of Carinthia, the beautiful banks of the blue Danube? How very few people know the *puzsta*, the immense plains of Hungary; and who has explored the wildernesses of Galicia and Transylvania, or the wonderful beauty of the Dalmatian coasts from the Bocche di Cattaro up to here, where we are on the shores of the Adriatic Sea? And just here—this little spot so full of memories and classic associations—who has ever heard even the names of Istria and the Littoral? And yet how pretty and interesting the scenery is in this unknown part of Austria. The azure waters of the Adriatic, the wonderful southern sky, the Italian landscapes, the many relics of old Roman life and grandeur, everything combines to make this country worthy to be seen and admired. Do you know," she concluded, "you ought to write a book about it."

"Write a book!" I exclaimed, duly horrified,— "I, who hate even to write a letter of ten lines!"

"Writing a book is quite different, I am sure," was the answer; "and I don't mean a learned, scientific work. Write a simple sketch of this part of the country. Begin with Duino, where we are now. Then we will make excursions to other places near here, and you can write about them. If you will do it, I will try to make the illustrations."

This was another thing; and though our host looked rather gloomy at the idea of having any book-writing going on under his roof (a thing decidedly against his principles), I promised I would think about it. At first I felt very much as an unhappy being feels who is about to make his first speech; he knows there are lots of things to be

Introduction

said, but for the life of him he cannot remember what they are.

Now, however, I have written the Introduction and made the first plunge. I am writing the rest to please my collaborator and myself. I do not intend to be apologetic. If other people like this scribble, all well and good; if they do *not*, they should not read it.

CASTLE DUINO

CHAPTER I

DUINO

Hast thou seen that lordly castle,
 That Castle by the Sea?
Golden and red above it
 The clouds float gorgeously.
               LONGFELLOW.

I NEVER read an account of any pile of stones, dignified by the name of "castle" and situated near the sea, that did not begin with these lines of Longfellow's. It is not the force of example, however, that makes me prefix them to this attempt at a description of one, but it is the fact that they really suit Duino.

It looks lordly and imposing enough standing out grand and massive on frowning cliffs two hun-

DUINO FROM THE SEA

dred feet above the sea, grim and gray, like some old sentinel keeping a constant watch over the blue waters of the Adriatic stretching at its feet.

The view from it is magnificent: before you the open sea; on both sides, extending in graceful curves, the coast, amethyst-hued; far on the left the white houses of Trieste, and rather nearer, the Imperial Castle of Miramar; on the right, just on the horizon, the tower of Aquileia, famous in Roman times; and in the dim distance the snow-clad Alps.

From the land side the castle looks perhaps even more stern and severe, and like the fortress it was in old days. Not a window is to be seen, only the bare fortifications and the old walls clad with ivy, almost as old to all appearance as the walls themselves.

What appeals to one most is the restfulness and quiet of the place. The old castle, with its towers and battlements, its cloisters and courtyard, stands just as it has stood for centuries. You are out of the world here, the bustling, hurrying, work-a-day world of to-day, and back again in a world of two or three hundred years ago.

It is a nice, sad sort of feeling that comes over one: you think of your debts, of the friends of your youth that are dead and gone, of your elderly relation from whom you have expectations, and who will *not* die, and other melancholy things of a like nature; but your troubles seem far away, and are quite pleasant—"grateful and comforting."

The place seems peopled with ghosts—ghosts of a bygone age. There is a legend that on certain nights of the year a troop of phantom horsemen ride into the courtyard, and even in daylight you almost expect something of the sort to happen—you

DOOR-KNOCKER

listen for the clank of arms and the ring of the horses' hoofs. Modern dress seems out of place, you feel you ought to be in armour yourself. Every nook and corner, every stone, seems to have a story to tell. What a pity they cannot speak and tell all they have seen!

The castle must have been well-nigh impregnable in the old days, and probably extended to the ruin one sees on the right, on entering it.

Between the two—the ruin and the inhabited part—there is a sort of half garden, half wilderness, known as the "Riviera"—a delightful spot. Ilex, cypresses, laurels, and olive-trees grow in luxuriant profusion. Little winding paths tempt you to explore them. There is a long, old, steep flight of steps with the trees meeting over them in a roof of green leaves, leading down to the sea. Old-fashioned flowers abound, and grow almost wild—purple irises, great blue periwinkles, honey-scented "dragons' mouths," and roses of every kind. Butterflies that are rare in England are common enough here—huge yellow swallow-tails, the graceful "White Admiral," glorious "Camberwell Beauties" flit from flower to flower. There are swarms of nightingales; and pigeons and starlings have formed a perfect colony in the cliff under the ruin; a pair of kestrels have their nest here too. There are snakes in the long grass, and bright-coloured lizards bask in the sunshine.

Notice the big doors as you enter the castle—there is "Salve!" on one of them. It is pleasant to know one is "welcome," but one always is in Austria—it is the land of hospitality.

On the other door is an ancient knocker—interesting if you have a passion for old things. That

BOREAS

ugly face over the archway is a portrait of Mr. Boreas, the personification of the North Wind. He is represented as continually blowing. As a matter of fact he does blow rather strongly here, and in the spring almost perpetually.

One of the most picturesque parts of the castle is

the old courtyard, with its big square tower, its glistening statues, its dark cloisters, its graceful balconies, and with the ivy entwining and creeping over everything. The tower is said to be Roman. There are rooms here that have been walled up for centuries and are so still—nobody knows why. It is said in the village too that somewhere in the tower is "the buried treasure." I should very much like to find *that!*

Those coats of arms in mosaic on the wall of the covered passage are the arms of some of the various owners of Duino. "Ditthalm, 1139," is the earliest date there. War was the principal amusement of those times, and these first "Lords of Duino" certainly had enough of it. It mattered little to them which side they were on. If there were a war, or a petty feud, or anything going on in which hard blows might be struck, there they were, on one side or the other. They must have been fine fellows in their way, these old warriors, and have kept the citizens of Trieste and the neighbouring little towns in a perpetual state of alarm.

Here I had written some beautiful sentiments about the chivalry and loyalty and manliness of "the men of old." I felt rather pleased with my handiwork. It was full of nice poetic sentences, with a dash of enthusiasm, and here and there a fine con-

THE ROMAN TOWER

tempt for our "degenerate time." So I went to my collaborator and wanted her appreciation. I cannot say she *did* appreciate my flight of eloquence

—I did not find her quite so enthusiastic as I had expected.

"Don't be so ridiculous," she exclaimed. "What do we know about the men of old? I have not the slightest respect for them. I am sure they were exactly as men are now—if anything I think they were worse; but I don't know anything about it, and you don't either, so please stop that nonsense and stick to the present times—they may be 'degenerate,' but they are much more comfortable."

No, I decidedly think she was *un*sympathetic!

. . . . .

Duino changed hands many times. In 1465 it was the property of the Emperor Frederick III., and in 1508 it belonged to the city of Venice. In 1669 it came into the possession of the Della Torre (the old Lords of Milan), and from them it descended to Prince Egon-Carl Hohenlohe, the father of the present owner, our host.

There is a portrait of Dante in the covered passage. He came to visit Pagano Della Torre here about the year 1320, and is said to have frequented the little island near the bathing place in the "Riviera." The neighbourhood of Duino was very different in his time from what it is now; tradition says the hills were covered with forests of red pine, and that the country generally was swarming with game. The game now is conspicuous by its absence; there is one solitary hare left, which inhabits Dante's island, by the way.

Poor old Dante! He looks very melancholy and unhappy, but we can most of us sympathise with him. There are not many of us, however easily the wheels of life may have run, who do not feel a pang of something like regret when now and then the thought of some one gone out of our lives comes over us. Fate plays tricks with us all. Death, the force of circumstances—it matters little what the cause of our separation was; we have drifted apart, and there is nothing left us but a memory—a dream of what might have been.

CHAPTER II

DUINO—*continued*

> Full of long-sounding corridors it was,
>   That over-vaulted grateful gloom,
> Thro' which the livelong day my soul did pass,
>   Well pleased, from room to room.
>   TENNYSON.

THE covered passage before mentioned leads one straight to the principal staircase. It is a graceful winding staircase, and rare and interesting prints cover the walls. On the first landing, after passing through two anterooms (the second of which contains a collection of fine old Viennese china), one enters the dining-room. It is a large room with a balcony, from which there is a beautiful view of Miramar and the sea. There are some most appropriate pictures of eatables by various Dutch masters on the walls. It was a curious taste of these gentlemen to paint things to eat. Perhaps they were on the verge of starvation—that might account for it. I should have thought they might have found more interesting studies, though, than "gralloched" hares

THE BALCONY

and fishes with their necks broken. I know nothing of Art (this is constantly dinned into me), so can speak absolutely without prejudice. An old telescope that once belonged to Nelson, and was presented by him to Count Della Torre (Thurn), Admiral of the King of Naples, is in this room. It is a very good glass; one can see things through it almost as well as with the naked eye, but it requires some manipulation to get the focus right.

People dine well in Austria, but you get a superabundance of veal. Veal for lunch, veal for dinner, veal cooked in many ways and concealed under numerous devices, but always veal. There is a fearful invention called "Schnitzl" that is the worst form of all. Foreigners say we English live on beef and mutton, but in Austria they live on veal, so we have the pull over them in the way of variety. One never sees grown-up cattle here. Poor things! they don't get the chance of reaching years of maturity, they are always killed in the first spring of their youth.

Opening into the dining-room is a small drawing-room. This contains mostly family portraits. The most noticeable among them is the portrait of the late Princess Hohenlohe. She must have been very beautiful, and has a very English appearance. She was the last Della Torre.

There are two pictures here that I am convinced are by Morland. No one knew this before, so I am very proud at having made the discovery. Some other animal pictures are ascribed to a Venetian artist

—Longhi—portraits of horses. They are extraordinary horses—very fat, and they appear to have been taught to beg, as they are almost all standing up on their hind legs. I am told this is a playful habit that Spanish steeds had.

You go up another flight of stairs and arrive at the door of the gallery. This is a long passage, especially designed for ghosts to walk in—not the sort of place one would care to be left alone in after dark. There are some very fine pictures of the Venetian and Dutch schools here. One of the best is the "Entrance of the Dogaressa Morosina Morosini into Venice," by Tintoretto—all the figures are said to be portraits. At the further end of the gallery is the great banqueting hall. There is a portrait here by Van Dyck of one Matthew Hofer, a former owner of Duino. An old chronicle calls him "a tempestuous and arrogant youth, who had always his hand on his sword, and whose whole life was a drama of blood." In his portrait he has a proud and handsome face, with dark melancholy eyes.

The other full-length portraits represent some of the Lords of Milan—Della Torre—who after many years of unending civil wars were vanquished by the rival family, the Visconti, and obliged to fly from

Milan. They took refuge near their kinsman, Pagano IV., then Patriarch of Aquileia, and soon gained wealth and great power in their adopted country. They

PORTRAIT OF MATTHEW HOFER (Van Dyck)

were a turbulent and overbearing race, and many are the tales still told by the people of their violent or heroic deeds.

Notice the painting of the gentleman on the

THE BANQUETING HALL

ferocious-looking horse, that appears determined to

jump on you whichever part of the room you retire to. He was quite a character, and had a special talent for eloping with other people's wives. On one occasion he was condemned to be beheaded, and the soldiers of the Emperor were sent to Duino to arrest him. He treated them with great hospitality, and gave them a splendid banquet—probably in this very room. After dinner he retired to his own apartment, and as all the entrances to the castle were securely guarded, the unsuspicious soldiers thought nothing of it. Suddenly they heard a shot from the sea, rushed to find out what it was, and perceived their former prisoner on board a ship in full sail. Our friend fired the shot to let his would-be captors know they need not wait for him—a proof of his kindly and considerate nature! There was an underground passage leading from the library (the entrance may still be seen) to the shore. The soldiers did not know this, and their host had omitted to inform them of the fact.

It is said that he was retaken years afterwards and deprived of his head; but there is another account that he made a compact with the devil and escaped again, this time on a black horse, one of His Satanic Majesty's own particular breed, that carried him safely over the sea to Aquileia, where horse and rider disappeared, and were seen no more.

The old man on the gray steed who is so cruelly trampling down four poor individuals very scantily clothed, is Napoleon I. Della Torre. One story says he rode over his own children in this way, but it is a base calumny; the children are four cities which he conquered for Milan, allegorically represented in the picture.

In the library I examined the entrance to the famous underground passage. You see a trap-door cleverly concealed in the wooden floor, and on lifting it, a small staircase leads you down to a very diminutive room, built in the thickness of the massive outer wall. On your left is the passage. It is very small—in fact, you have to proceed on your hands and knees, and after a few yards you are stopped by a quantity of stones and earth.

The father of "our host" wished to have the old passage reopened, and set people to work, but it seems they were so frightened at finding a number of human bones mixed with the soil and rubbish, that it was impossible to persuade them to work on. They said it would be dangerous to clear it, as the castle would inevitably fall in consequence—a mere excuse, of course. I think the mysterious passage must descend through the terrace tower which rises against the middle of the side of the castle that faces the sea, and come out somewhere in the " Riviera," meeting the old staircase spoken of in the preceding chapter.

THE RIVIERA

I must say this passage interested me much more than all the many books of the library, but I noticed an enormous old " missal," most elaborately painted by hand on parchment, a very valuable work of the fifteenth century.

There is a charming little recess in the library,

where there are some beautiful miniatures, one or two fine old pastels, and some splendid old china; this corner would be a paradise for an antiquary.

A RECESS IN THE LIBRARY

A portrait of "Martin the Giant," a big man clad in armour, looks down threateningly from one of the dark corners of the room. He was a great warrior and statesman in his native Lombardy, but finally went off to the Crusades, and after showing great prowess, is said to have been taken and skinned alive by the Saracens (1147).

The walls of the drawing-room, next to the library, are covered with pictures, mostly of religious subjects. I suppose I ought to expatiate on them, but the artistic side of my nature is exhausted, and I should probably admire the wrong ones.

What I can safely speak of is the view from the large terrace over the afore-mentioned tower, where we used to have breakfast. It was charming to sit there in the early morning and look out upon that grand expanse of boundless sea, with the little wavelets dancing in the sunshine; it was almost cool too at that time of the morning.

. . . . .

Here the "energetic lady" remarks in an undertone that at this early hour she believes I was generally in bed, and that she did not remember having *once* seen me at breakfast on the terrace. Fortunately I can allow such remarks to pass unnoticed.

. . . . .

There is a mysterious charm about all these old rooms, they are so quiet, so restful, with their stained floors, their black oak carving, the tapestried hangings, and the old furniture. There are no bright colours, everything is subdued; no glare, always a sombre half-light. One feels inclined to walk softly in them, and speak in whispers, so as not to disturb their restfulness. There is something almost sad about their silence; they belong to a time long ago, not to the present day, and they seem to be waiting—waiting for the years that have passed to come again.

CHAPTER III

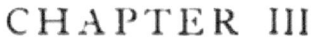IRAMAR

> And round about his home the glory
>   That blushed and bloomed
> Is but a dim-remembered story
>   Of the old time entombed.
> E. A. Poe.

On Friday, 31st May, we all went to Miramar, eleven of us. We drove to Nabresina, the nearest station to Duino, went from there to Miramar by train (it gave some trouble to the engine-driver, as he had to stop the train on purpose for us to get out), and then walked from the station to the castle. It was a stupid way of getting there; it would have been much better to have driven all the way, but the directress of our party did not think so. I suppose she thought we should enjoy the various modes of travelling. It was rather a pity we had not relays of saddle-horses and bicycles to meet us somewhere—we should have had still more variety. We might have crawled the last bit too on our hands and knees, but I didn't think of it at the time. I used to like railway travelling. When I was very small I could have no greater treat than to be taken somewhere by train—now I don't. I still like to *see* a train. If I am in the country and feel lonely, I walk to the nearest railway line and wait for an express to rush by. That cheers me. I don't wish to be in it—the sight of it is enough. It must be an English express, however; a Continental express merely irritates one, and deepens the melancholy; I feel I can walk faster than it can travel.

We arrived at the Imperial Castle at last. The gardens are very pretty. There are numbers of terraces, and flights of steps, and cedar-trees, and little Italian gardens. There are big palm-trees, and strange foreign-looking shrubs, and beautiful beds of old-fashioned monthly roses.

. . . . .

I had written so far in this chapter when I thought I had better consult my collaborator. I found her making a sketch in pen and ink. "That is very nice," I said. "I really know those things are trees."

"I am glad you realise what they are," she answered with icy coldness. "Won't you read what you have written?"

I did so, and then the storm burst.

"You call *that* a description of those beautiful gardens!" she said. "Have you no poetry in your nature? Have you no appreciation of the beautiful? Why don't you say much more of the terraces, the marble staircases? Why don't you speak of the funereal cypresses clear-cut against the sky, the dark green of the ilex contrasting with the gray of the olives? Why don't you write about the white starry blossom of the jasmine, the sweet scent of the honey-suckle, the tea-roses creeping up and festooning the rough stems of the towering palm-trees, and shedding their perfume on the soft summer air, the glistening of the water in the fountains, the azure blue of the sea, the whiteness of the marble statues gleaming through the dark foliage, the mysterious appearance of the Italian gardens with their staircases leading down to the deep-hued waters of the Adriatic? Why don't you say something about the liquid notes of the nightingale, the faint whispering of the trees overhead, the 'Lovers' Walk?' Oh! you *are* stupid."

Perhaps I am. I have written all I could remember of our conversation. I hope she will be satisfied now.

. . . . .

The castle was built about the middle of the present century by the Emperor Maximilian. We

MIRAMAR

saw the rooms that had been his. They are built to exactly resemble the cabins on board his ship when he was Admiral of the Austrian Fleet. Every one knows his tragic story: how he, persuaded by the promise of French support, went off to be Emperor of Mexico; how the French deserted him (France has done many things she may well be ashamed of, but nothing more dastardly than this); how he was captured by the rebel Mexicans, and finally shot by them. Poor fellow! one would have thought that with all he had he might have been content without being Emperor of Mexico. But who knows what dreams of glory and heroic adventures passed through his brain! He was a poet and an enthusiast, a man worshipped by the people, and in his veins flowed the blood of Charles V., who once had been the master of those far countries where his destiny called him. And what must have been his thoughts when he, the son of the German Cæsars, stood forsaken and betrayed before the handful of rebels who put an end to all his golden dreams? In any case his end was worthy of his noble nature. There is an incident in connection with it not generally known. One of the few Mexicans who remained faithful to him was Mejia, one of his generals. He was also captured by the rebels, and was condemned to be shot with the Emperor, but with this difference: for the Emperor a company of picked shots had been selected, and for Mejia they had chosen a number of raw and young recruits, unaccustomed to the use of the rifle. The Emperor, whose experienced eye had immediately remarked the cruel intention of the Mexicans, ordered his companion, as the last boon he could grant him, to exchange places with him. Mejia obeyed, and was killed instantaneously ; but the Emperor died a lingering and miserable death.

People say he was so disfigured that when his embalmed body arrived in Vienna, no one, not even the Grand Master of the Court, could be quite sure of his identity.

I do not admire the castle. It is new, and looks new, and is built in no particular style, though the first intention was evidently to make it Gothic. One sees the love of the unfortunate Emperor for Spanish and Moorish things, by the way in which they are dotted here and there. The interior too is rather tasteless. There are some fine things, but the arrangement is bad. A beautiful cabinet that once belonged to Marie Antoinette is in one of the rooms ; it has some wonderful old Wedgwood china on the doors.

We were shown round by the most melancholy attendant it has ever been my lot to meet with. He seemed to find it a heartrending business, and his voice sounded as if he were continually on the verge of tears. I was quite glad when the inspection was over. I am tender-hearted myself, and do not like to wantonly distress any one.

After viewing the castle we went out into the gardens again, and (I am sorry to have to confess it) ate some provisions that we had brought with us, on one of the flights of marble steps. Then we wandered about in the gloaming till it was time for our train.

It was a lovely evening :—

> Skies strewn with roses fading, fading slowly,
> While one star, trembling, watched the daylight die.

The nightingale's rich music and the soft murmur of the waves were the only sounds. All the clamour and bustle of the day were over. The moon rose and flooded the calm sea with a pathway of melted silver; the stars came out one by one, and seemed to smile on us. It was the time when all evil thoughts go out of one's heart, when heaven itself seems nearer in the dim light. On such an evening I always think of the old familiar words of the " blessing " after the sermon, " The peace of God, which passeth all understanding."

We had an exciting adventure during our return journey in the train. We had started, and the conductor was just examining our tickets—having carefully left the door open—when the Vienna " express " crawled by (I almost said *tore*, but I cannot tell a lie). Some projecting portion of it caught our carriage door, sent it to with a violent crash, smashing the door and half tearing it from its hinges. The crash was like a cannon-shot, and the explosion was followed by the tinkling of the shower of broken glass that

THE RISING MOON

fell over and around us. For the moment we could

not understand what had happened, and all looked fearfully around, expecting to see pieces of ourselves lying about the wrecked compartment. Fortunately, we were all whole and unhurt, however. Of course, there was the wildest excitement in our railway carriage. "The Seal" kept congratulating himself on not having been nearer the broken window, and explaining what dreadful injuries would have ensued for him if he had been. The directress of our party — the "Energetic Lady"— abused an unfortunate stationmaster, who came at the next stoppage to inquire about the accident, in such a way that the poor man shrank back terrified and in tears. The "Learned Fair Man" started a scientific theory (in which he dragged in Darwin) to explain the matter; but the "Learned Dark Man" (with Schopenhauer in the background) had another scientific explanation exactly the reverse. The "Fat Boy" thought Anarchists had an especial grudge against himself; the "Thin Boy" profited by the occasion to bleed copiously from the nose—a pastime he had indulged in at intervals throughout the whole day, and the other boy lost immediately the one bag of the party. The two other ladies, who had not been in the baneful compartment, explained at great length all their misgivings, presentiments, and extraordinary perceptions ; whilst my collaborator shrieked excitedly—

"There! that's a beautiful incident for the book."

"Bother the book!" I answered with pensive grace.

After this the drive home was dull and uneventful. We were almost smothered in dust, but that was merely a trifling inconvenience, which the beauty of the night and the glorious moonlight quite made up for.

CHAPTER IV

THE TIMAVO AND SAN GIOVANNI

> O water whispering
> Still through the dark into mine ears.
>
> D. G. Rossetti.

I MADE two excursions to the Timavo and San Giovanni. The first was with the "Fat Boy." It was a rainy sort of day, and there was nothing to be done in the way of exercise but to go for a walk, so I beguiled the "Fat Boy" into accompanying me. I like to take him for walks. I feel I am doing good to suffering humanity—he may get rid of a little of his superfluous flesh by the exertion. I cannot say that up to now he has exhibited much thankfulness for my philanthropic efforts. We took Pixner, the gamekeeper, and his two dogs with us. Pixner is much looked up to in the village of Duino as a great traveller and linguist. He spent one or two years in England as servant to "our host," and was commonly known there as "Mr. Pig-nose"—his own name being found difficult to pronounce.

San Giovanni is not far from Duino—only a walk of half an hour or so. It is classic ground, for does not the world-famed Timavo make here its appearance into the light of day?

> Antenor potuit mediis elapsus Achivis
> Illyricos penetrare sinus atque intima tutus
> regna Liburnorum et fontem superare Timavi,
> unde per ora novem vasto cum murmure montis
> it mare proruptum et pelago premit arva sonanti.
> VIRGIL'S *Aeneid*, Book I. 242-246.

The "nine mouths" of Virgil have now sunk to three, however. It is a most extraordinary thing, this river, all at once, seeming to come from nowhere, there it is, not a little feeble, trickling streamlet, but a wide, fast-flowing river. There is no doubt that the original springs are somewhere underground, and that it runs for a considerable distance in the bowels of the earth. Every now and then on the neighbouring hill-side you come to a hole in the ground where you hear the rush of the water, and the splash if you drop a stone down.

The ground about this neighbourhood is a perfect honeycomb.

Almost all the classic authors speak of the Timavo. I had carefully compiled a list of these old gentlemen with a kind of history of the river, but I will spare

SPRINGS OF THE TIMAVO

the reader, and merely say that they believed it to be the entrance to the Infernal Regions, and that the Argonauts are said to have come here after they had annexed the Golden Fleece.

After having gazed at the place where the Timavo first appears, we went on to the little church of San

Giovanni. This is very old, and is built on the foundations of a temple erected by the Greeks in honour of Diomed—either the Greek hero or the Thracian Diomed who was celebrated for his horses. The latter gentleman seems to have had a stud in the neighbourhood of San Giovanni. The horses from this part of the country were very celebrated, and eagerly sought after for the Olympian games. It is interesting to note that one of the great annual events here is the horse-fair of Duino, which takes place in the month of June.

The Romans built a temple on the same site later on, the temple of the "Speranza Augusta"; and there was another temple—that of the Nymphs—somewhere near it. Villas and country houses were here in abundance; it was then quite a fashionable watering-place on account of the warm springs in the neighbourhood. There is still a miserable little bathing-place at some distance from San Giovanni, a most abandoned and dismal-looking house, though the waters have still their ancient reputation for great healing power.

In Roman times the view from this now solitary spot must have been very beautiful: the murmuring springs of the Timavo, the great lake (now a marsh), with its banks bright with glistening white monuments, and the neighbouring boundless forests, which fable said were inhabited by the most extraordinary creatures.

The wine of the country was very famous. It was the favourite beverage of Julia (or Livia), the wife of Augustus, who died in Aquileia at the age of eighty-three. She gave all the credit of her long life to the wine! Pliny the younger is our informant on this point.

Battles were continually fought on the Timavo towards the end of the Roman Empire and in the Middle Ages. Its banks were the scene of many a fierce conflict between the Roman legions and the Barbarians, whilst, later on, the German Emperors would generally choose this way to sweep down from the north upon Italy. The Venetian and Imperial troops often fought here, and the different lords of the land being always at war with each other, the country round about was kept pretty lively.

The "pigeon-holes" among the rocks are very interesting. They are like the shafts of extinct volcanoes, and descend to a great depth into the earth. The pigeons, which are identically the same bird as the old-fashioned English "Blue-rock," make their nests in the sides. There is good shooting to be had at these holes in September by lying in wait for the pigeons as they come home in the evening.

The second time we went by sea, in a diminutive cutter bearing the proud name of *St. George*. I dislike yachting on the whole — there is always either too much wind or none at all. In my case it is generally the latter. It is enough for me to go out in a yacht for a cruise of an hour or two, and you may be sure that yacht will become becalmed, and the unhappy people on board will have to choose between a night "on the ocean wave" and a row home in a small boat. I seem to be a sort of Jonah, and live in expectation of being thrown overboard every time I go on a yacht. A steamer does away with the fear of being becalmed, but then there is the smell of the engines. Do not mistake me, it is not that I fear sea-sickness,

> For I can weather the roughest gale
> That ever wind did blow.

In fact, I am an excellent sailor.

Once I did feel rather queer, but that was a dispensation of Providence in fulfilment of the old adage "Pride goes before a fall." I was crossing the Channel — Dover to Calais. We had a small steamer, a choppy sea, and there was a young man with a Kodak on board. I abominate amateur photographers. They are offensive. It is the fact that they insist on photography being an art that makes them so objectionable. Photography is *not* an art. One merely requires a good apparatus and a knowledge of how to work it, and there you are—a good photographer. That is *my* idea on the subject.

Well, this young man was *particularly* offensive. He wore a knickerbocker suit, and skipped about with his Kodak and took "snap-shots" at everything. He did not "speak to the man at the wheel," but he "shot" him instead. He photographed the sea, the sky, the sea-gulls, the passing steamers, his fellow-passengers; but then he became sea-sick. His Kodak fell from his nerveless hand, and he looked very ill. I revelled in his misery, I "chortled in my joy"; but the Fates were on my track. Half an hour before we reached Calais I began to feel very miserable. I thought I was dying. Somebody came to me, a sailor, or a steward, or an admiral, or something of that sort, and asked me if I felt ill. I said I did, that my last hour had come, that I wanted to throw myself overboard and hasten the end. He would not let me do this. I should feel all right when we landed, he said. I knew this was impossible, it was merely uselessly lengthening my sufferings; but, curiously enough, he was right. At the time I was unable to understand my misery, but I see through it now. My wretchedness was intended to teach me a lesson—the lesson of never laughing at people in adversity. I learnt it, and since then have never suffered evil effects from being on the sea.

This is a long digression, but I wish to explain the disgust I felt on our going to San Giovanni by sea. We were not becalmed on this occasion, but there was next to no wind, the sun was blazing hot, and as we were constantly tacking, and the *St. George* is a very small boat, my life was in perpetual danger from the eccentricities of the boom. I was very unhappy, and not in the mood to admire the beauties of nature that were constantly pointed out to me. But Checco was a comfort. Checco is captain, crew, and cabin-boy combined of the *St. George*, a great character and a philosopher. A nice-looking man too, tall and broad-shouldered, with a bronzed skin and snowy white hair (though, in fact, he is not old) and extraordinarily bright blue eyes—they look as if all the light and colour of the sea were reflected in them. He is a proud man is Checco, and generally very silent. He only talks to particular chums, but then he *does* talk. The "Fat Boy" is the proud possessor of his confidence, and to him Checco unfolds his theories; he even puts the two learned men in the shade with regard to theories. On this particular occasion he was explaining earthquakes. (There have been some here lately.) This is what Checco said to the "Fat Boy": "People are very much afraid of earthquakes, you know. I am not afraid, for it is no use. What must be, must be. But I say, What is the reason for them? I will tell you: it is the doing of those mad winds. When I was young, things were quite different on the sea. The winds blew steadily. Either it was Bora, or Levante, or Scirocco, or Libeccio, and you knew how long it would blow in the same direction. It was a pleasure to sail a boat *then*. But now the winds blow all ways at once, and are always fighting against one another. The weaker winds *must* give way, and what becomes of *them?* They rush into the earth—you know all the holes and grottoes there are everywhere—and so cause the earthquakes. Yes, you can believe me, it is all the doing of those mad winds." Checco was silent and gazed out over the blue sea, and the "Fat Boy" pondered over his words. Then he began again, still looking at the distant horizon: "Everything

CASTLE DUINO FROM THE ROMAN ROAD

was different when I was a young man—the winds were not mad, the girls *were* pretty. When we came out of church on Sundays, and the girls, as is the fashion, gave the red carnation they wore to the man they liked best, none of the fellows got as many as I did. But now I have white hair, you see. . . . Still none of my boys are as tall as I am, and I have never tried my whole strength yet."

Then Checco relapsed into silence, and not even the "Fat Boy" could draw another word from him.

. . . . .

We sailed up the Timavo. The wind had freshened, and I must confess it was really rather pleasant. Wild ducks rose from the reeds with a great splashing and flapping of wings, and occasionally a snipe would dart away with its peculiar twisting zigzag flight and harsh cry. At San Giovanni we landed, and walked home. Our path, for part of the way, lay along an old Roman road, and then we passed through a little wood of stunted trees (the last remnant of the "boundless forests" of old times), which in autumn is one pink carpet of heavily-scented cyclamens. We skirted the deer park, where some twenty or thirty fallow deer lead a cheerless existence and are fed on hay all the year round. The ground in the park is covered with stones, not a blade of grass is to be seen, only the hardy ilex seems able to flourish on the barren soil.

It has a curious appearance, this little tract of country round Duino, with its dull gray rocks. A few bushes manage to extract enough nourishment from somewhere to exist, but every cranny and crevice in the stones is gay and bright with wild flowers.

Monotonous and almost melancholy is the scenery, and yet it has a charm of its own; the sun shines so brightly, the sky is so blue; and then there is always the sea, ever changeful and ever beautiful, and the old gray castle in the distance, towering above all, and watching over the silent land.

CHAPTER V

RAINY DAY

> The rain came down upon my head
> Unsheltered, and the heavy wind
> Rendered me mad, and deaf, and blind.
>   E. A. Poe.

It was not quite so bad as all that. I did not go out in the rain, and at present I am neither deaf nor blind. I cannot be sure about the madness. It was very wet, though, but it cleared up before the evening.

A really wet day may be dreary, but still it is rather pleasant to have one sometimes. The rain affords such a grand excuse to be idle and do nothing. One can lounge about, and smoke, and read the newspapers or a novel all day, and justly feel it is quite impossible to be energetic. I am often told that my besetting sin is laziness. I am not sure whether it is true, but all I can say is, it is very pleasant to spend a lazy day occasionally. One must have piles of work waiting to be done, or it loses its charm. If there is really nothing to do, one is bored, and wants something to fill up the time.

On this particular day, however, I was not lazy—far from it. We explored the castle thoroughly from dungeon to attic, with a view to discovering new beauties for "the book."

I must say that occasionally I almost repent of my rashness in promising to write this book; my collaborator is so intensely business-like, and keeps me at it from early morn till dewy eve. I never have a moment's rest. It somewhat detracts too from the pleasure of going anywhere to know that you have to write an account of everything you see afterwards.

We began with the "grotto room." This is a summer drawing-room that we usually sit in. It is a big room, with a tiled floor and an arched roof; the latter and the walls are of cement, thickly studded with little bits of stalactite, that glisten and gleam when the place is lighted up, and give a fairy-like appearance to it. Birds of paradise and sea-gulls, suspended by invisible wires, swing from the vaulted roof and appear to be hovering about the room.

Enormous shells, quaint Venetian lamps and mirrors, funny old china, are scattered all about. There is a curious old sedan chair standing in one corner, and

THE GROTTO ROOM

near it are two pianos. I never made out the mystery of those two pianos. I believe they are near relations, and that they would be heart- (or string-) broken if they were to be separated. There is a massive marble mantelpiece at the farther end, surmounted by two shields, one bearing the Hohenlohe leopards, and the other the tower and crossed lilies of the Della Torre. Altogether it is a quaint room, without any particular order or style, but very comfortable, and it has one great advantage in being cool. I have spent many a weary hour here, labouring over these sketches, or gazing out through the coloured glass at the sea and the glorious sunsets.

The sunsets at Duino are magnificent—the whole western sky is one flaming blaze of colour, of every tint, from the deepest crimson to the faintest daffodil. The most beautiful moment is, I think, when the sun has sunk to rest behind the distant Alps, that stand out pearly-gray against the rose-coloured sky, and the sea in the foreground glows like a huge bowl of melted gold.

We went next to see the dungeons. They are by no means cheerful — two little damp and musty rooms, destitute of furniture, with grated windows and enormously thick walls—you see their immense thickness when you enter. The last man who was confined here (it was not so very long ago) hung himself. He is now said to haunt them. Poor fellow! one cannot wonder that he should have availed himself of the only possible way of escape open to him.

We then penetrated a little room where the family archives are kept. It has a massive iron door, and shelves full of dusty, musty old parchments. We unearthed a grand treasure here—an old manuscript diary of a tour through France and Italy at the beginning of this century, written by an Englishman of the name of Cockburn. Fired by this discovery we rushed up the tower stairs to another little room, formerly used as a study by an old priest who had once belonged to the household. We found it just as he had left it : the chair, the pens, the old inkbottle, and he, poor old man, dead years ago! He wrote a book in Italian about Duino and the neighbourhood. It has been very useful to us in some respects, though it is very confused.

We came down the tower stairs again, and I was shown the door of the walled-up rooms ; it has been carefully built up flush with the wall, and recently whitewashed over, so as to conceal it. Then we explored all the funny little staircases and passages that are everywhere about the castle, and form a perfect labyrinth.

The rain had cleared off by this time, and the sun was struggling to show himself through the clouds, so we went out, the "Other Boy" accompanying us. First we went down into the old moat, long dry and overgrown with grass and nettles, but in one corner some white lilies rise pure and stately, and bloom unseen in this neglected spot. Some fragments of Roman columns have been built into the wall of the castle—one sees them from the moat. Then we explored some terraces that are round the outside walls, where enormous yellow roses cling to the crumbling stones and lemon-scented verbenas grow wild. We made another interesting discovery here—at least it would be interesting if the general opinion about it is correct. We found a hole in the wall of the tower under the terrace. My collaborator maintains it is the beginning of a ventilating shaft that communicates with the underground passage, but I am afraid it is nothing but a rat-hole.

We descended some rickety stairs, and after inspecting a sculptured Madonna, who, half overgrown with ivy, looks down on the occasional passers-by (people admire her; I do *not*, as she has her nose on one side), proceeded to the battlements. There are two old field-pieces here that formerly belonged to the French Republic. They have the *fasces* engraved upon them and the inscription, " An VII. République francaise 6 Fructidor." I could not discover the history of these guns. I was told a hazy story about Duino being in the hands of the French in the beginning of this century ; of its being stormed,

CASTLE DUINO FROM THE MOAT

taken, and partially burnt by the English, and that

the English captain was always drunk ; but the story lacks confirmation—particularly the last part of it.

In any case, the French were here, and took away all the contents of the armoury. In 1813, too, Trieste being in the possession of the French, Admiral Freemantle sailed up the Adriatic with some English men-of-war, whilst General Nugent advanced on the land side with the Austrian troops. The French commander retired into the citadel, and was there besieged by the English and Austrians. On October 24th the French surrendered.

This being so, it is quite possible that there was a siege of Duino, as it is very strongly situated and has always been an object for attack. Even as recently as 1866, in the war between Austria and Italy, the Italians had intended to land at Duino, had not their fleet been destroyed in the battle of Lissa.

We went down the old staircase to the little bathing-place near Dante's island. There is a strong wire net in the water to guard against the sharks. "Our host" disapproves of this net. He maintains that if any one bathing at Duino is unfortunate enough to be eaten by the one solitary shark that cruises in the Adriatic, he or she is the victim of such extraordinary bad luck that it is much better for him or her to be finished off at once.

A Rainy Day 59

Then we wandered through the " Riviera " to the

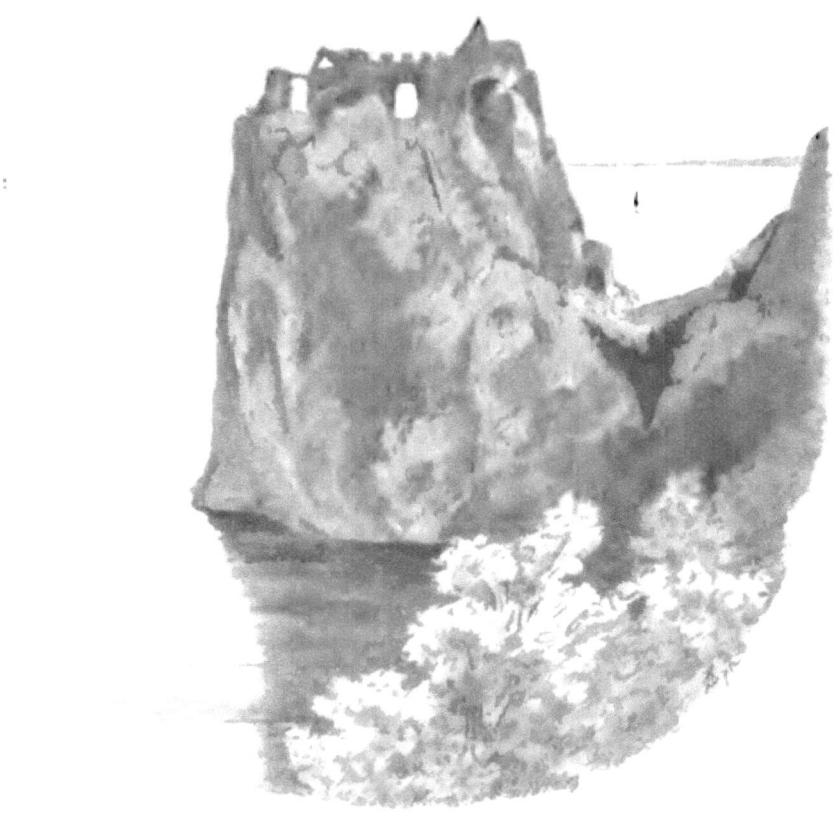

THE RUIN

old ruin and the little sombre wood "sacred to

Diana." The ruined castle rises dark and threatening on a massive and perpendicular rock, which is on three sides surrounded by the sea. The position is immensely strong—one can only approach by one little narrow path that could easily have been held in the old days by two or three resolute men. There is not much to be seen in the ruin. It is all crumbling to pieces and is half-smothered with creepers and grass. In one vaulted arch, probably once part of the chapel, there are faint traces of fresco-painting; and there are one or two enormous stone bullets lying about that must have been thrown from some kind of catapult. Every provision was made for a siege. One sees the old well, which still holds water.

Just under the old ruined castle the ground sinks and forms a hollow, and there a little wood of ilex-trees has grown, through whose dark and thick evergreen foliage no ray of sunlight seems ever to penetrate. It is a weird and uncanny sort of place: the trees seem black, the ground is black, and no grass or flowers grow there. Only on some bit of old crumbling masonry the ivy has extended a funereal pall. No birds seem to nestle in this solitary spot, and the earth smells damp, whilst you shiver a little in the cool shade of the sacred trees. It is peculiarly quiet and silent under the ilex; and if, sitting there in the long summer afternoons, you get drowsy and dreamy, thinking perhaps of times long, long ago, you would not wonder very much if, through the dark green of the melancholy trees that make a dome of shade over your head, a white form should glide, swift and silent—glide down from the golden light beyond into the darkness and gloom of the ilex wood.

Dream or reality, what does it matter, since both pass away in the night of time, and after a while are remembered no more?

How many may have come under the old, old ilex-trees in drowsy hot summer afternoons, or later, when the silver moon tried with her trembling rays to pierce the dark gloom of the wood! how many, each with his burden of joy or sorrow—gone—forgotten—faded away!

Dream or reality, what does it matter?

CHAPTER VI

QUILEIA

> We were a gallant company.
> BYRON.

ON Tuesday, 4th June, we had a regular "day out." We were twelve—the original eleven who went to Miramar, with the addition of "our host." We started at 7.30 in the morning, and this involved getting up at six. There is nothing I object to more than early rising. Since my earliest infancy I have always been told what an excellent thing it is to get up early, and the ancient proverb (which you may have heard)—

> Early to bed and early to rise
> Makes a man healthy, wealthy, and wise—

has been repeated to me so often that I actually know it by heart. I do not believe in it, though; I infinitely prefer the sentiments contained in the old Scotch song—

> I would rather go supperless to my bed
> Than rise in the morning early.

It was not a matter of going supperless to bed in this case, but it meant (at least to our host and myself—we were late) starting without breakfast. We rose to the occasion. Rather than keep the rest of the party waiting, we went without breakfast, and had the satisfaction of feeling martyrs for the rest of the day.

My collaborator, our host, the Thin Boy, and myself were in the first carriage. We kept congratulating ourselves and each other on this fact all the way. There was plenty of dust, clouds of it, and we could dimly discern the other carriages behind us, and their miserable occupants being half-smothered, whilst we were in the pure fresh air of the morning. It was a very pretty drive of about two hours to Aquileia, past marshy meadows bright with flowers, and vineyards with their graceful festoons of vines, the fresh and luxuriant green of the plain contrasting strangely with the gray barrenness of the neighbouring hills, through the little old-fashioned town of Monfalcone. It is quite an Italian town, with its big piazza, graceful church tower, and balconied houses—closely shuttered, of course; the inhabitants seem to have a horror of fresh air. After Monfalcone the scenery too becomes quite Italian, though we are still in Austria. The plain continues fresh and green as ever, but the hills fade away in the blue distance. We cross that bluest of rivers, the Isonzo, drive between green hedges fragrant with wild roses and honeysuckle, pass a long, low, house covered with roses, with a lovely garden and a grass lawn-tennis ground (the only grass court I have seen on the Continent), go over numerous little brooks that wind along under the dark shadow of overhanging bushes, and are generally haunted by promising families of downy yellow ducklings, and at last reach Aquileia.

Here we had what was a second breakfast to most of the party, of coffee and rolls. Our host did not eat anything. He said he couldn't eat when he had risen in "the middle of the night." It was a mild rebuke, but it passed unnoticed.

We intended to go to Grado before seeing Aquileia, so after this meal we sought our steamer, a launch that plies daily between the two places. It did not require much seeking, firstly, because it rested on the placid waters of the canal close to our "hotel," and, secondly, as it guided us to its whereabouts, with great consideration, by a series of most unearthly screams of the whistle, and by disgorging vast quantities of evil-smelling smoke.

The scenery is rather pretty after leaving Aquileia. High reeds and grass grow down to the water's edge, larks carol joyously in the sky, reed-warblers twitter among the rushes, and bright-hued dragonflies dart hither and thither. There is a smell of new-mown hay in the air (which causes the Fat Boy to sneeze thirty-seven times without stopping), and one sees the peasants at work, with the big, gentle, sleepy-looking oxen drawing the waggons. One soon leaves the canal behind, and comes out into numberless shallow lagoons of salt water, with dreary sandbanks, and lonely-looking posts to mark the deeper channels. There are a few dismal huts on some of the sandbanks, and in one place a church tower stands alone in its glory—the rest of the church has fallen down. We saw no living thing there except a solitary eagle. It is a desolate and melancholy sort of place, and I for one was very glad when we came out into "blue water" and Grado hove in sight. It forms a pretty picture, this little Venetian-like town, the blue sea, and the fleet of fishing boats with their brightly-coloured sails.

Grado is a sea-bathing place, or *would* be one, if anybody went there. The bathing sheds are a very imposing-looking building, there is an excellent sandy beach, the water is lukewarm, and drowning is quite impossible on account of its shallowness. What Grado wants is a good waking up. If the inhabitants were a little more speculative; if they

FISHING BOAT (BRAGOZZO)

would build a good hotel and open a railway line, etc., it might become a flourishing place. At present there is no accommodation for visitors, so no visitors go there. We bathed, of course, all of us, with the exception of the two learned men, who had different theories with regard to bathing, and who were disputing thereon. We enjoyed it very much, except the Seal, who did not take at all kindly to his native element, and found it cold; he evidently felt, too, that his life was in danger, as he explained to every-

GRADO—THE HARBOUR

one the dreadful end he might come to if a larger wave than usual were to carry him away.

After our bath we returned to the hotel, very hungry. Our lunch included a dish called Risotto, which, I am told, can only be made to perfection in this part of the world; it is very good. Owing to the bathing and the lunch, the latter being much prolonged by the voracious appetites of the "Seal" and the "Fat Boy," we had no time to see the town thoroughly, but we managed to make a hurried inspection of the church before our steamer left. It is a fine old building, with two rows of marble columns in the interior, the capitals of which are

THE CHURCH AT GRADO

all different, and remind one of those in the church of St. Mark at Venice. The Byzantine pulpit, a very old episcopal seat behind the altar, and some sarcophagi with inscriptions and carvings in a little courtyard near the church, are also interesting.

Our return journey to Aquileia was not exciting. We were all sleepy, and hot, and rather irritable. On reaching it we proceeded to the hotel, and refreshed ourselves with sundry cooling drinks, and then set out to view the town.

Aquileia was founded B.C. 183 or 181, after the second war against Hannibal. It was one of the twelve fortified towns built to repel the attacks of the Barbarians, and at the same time such towers as Duino, Monfalcone, and Sagrado were erected as watch-towers. Aquileia was a very extensive and important place under the Romans, and possessed a population of half a million. With the decline of the Roman power the glory of Aquileia departed. The town withstood many attacks from the Barbarians, but after a siege of some months it was finally burnt down and quite destroyed by the Huns under Attila. Some of the inhabitants escaped to Grado, and others sought refuge among the neighbouring lagoons.

There is a museum of Roman remains containing a collection of statues, pottery, glass, etc. The old glass is very beautiful, its colouring wonderful, and two of the many statues are particularly fine, one of a Venus or a nymph, very much mutilated, and an almost perfect one of the family of Tiberius. The rest of the statues and carvings, though interesting, did not seem to be of great artistic value, still I was struck by a fine mosaic pavement representing the rape of Europa.

When one reflects that all this collection has been made up of things (one could almost say) casually found, one can form some idea of the valuable treasures still left in the soil. Probably Aquileia could rival Pompeii or Herculaneum—in any case, it was a much more important place. In the last year or two some Austrian noblemen have begun to interest themselves in making excavations. It is to be hoped they will continue the work, and that successful results may follow.

After some time Aquileia was rebuilt, but not on the same extensive scale. It seems that Charlemagne came to the town for the sake of the hunting that was to be had in the big forests then existing round Isonzo and Timavo. Old chronicles say that wild boar, wild goats, and pheasants were the principal objects of pursuit, but unfortunately there is no record of the "bags." When one sees the general barrenness of the country now, it is difficult to believe it was once all one dense forest through which the great Emperor and his nobles chased the flying game, whilst the woodland rang with the deep music of the hounds.

The church is extremely old—it dates back to

1031—and the arches and pillars of the interior are very graceful. There is a most curious monument in the church—a sort of little temple of white marble surrounded by marble columns that support a modern wooden roof. The inside is quite empty—no trace of fittings left. What it was used for is a riddle not yet solved.

Very interesting is a small chapel with the tombs of the four Della Torre who were Patriarchs of Aquileia. The power of the Patriarchs lasted for fourteen centuries. They were not only very great Church dignitaries, but possessed immense secular influence, and in spite of their peaceful profession were brave warriors. The Lords of Duino were generally their firm allies. We read that when Bertram, Patriarch of Aquileia, defeated the troops of Goritz at Osoppo (1340) he himself celebrated mass in his camp in full armour, it being Christmas Eve. Hence arose the custom, long existing in this part of the country, that on that night the priest should bless the people with the cross of the sword. It was to visit one of the Della Torre, who lies buried here, that Dante in 1320 came to Duino, which was at that time a dependency of the Patriarch of Aquileia.

A crypt is under the church, containing the relics

of various saints. Formerly an immense treasure was there too, but it is said that about 1820 an organised band of some hundreds of people from Udine and Goritz made a raid on the church and stole all that was left of it. The most valuable part, and among other treasures a copy of the Gospel of St. Mark, written in the fifth century, had been taken away long before, and is to be seen now in the neighbouring town of Cividale, where the Patriarchs had in later time transported their seat. Some old Byzantine fresco-paintings of saints are at the east end, very much faded, but still discernible. On the roof above them are some hideous modern abominations. It is a great pity that in the last century all the old frescoes were whitewashed over, and in some places *repainted*. Now people are trying to discover the old paintings, but it will be a long and difficult task. The font is outside the church. It is enclosed in a circular wall, and is of unusual size — a relic of Roman times, as it seems.

We were completely exhausted after going round the town, and returned to the hotel with the ladies, clamouring for ices. I think we spent the greater part of this day in eating and drinking.

After all, it was an impression of sadness that I took with me as we left the town behind us. Turning round, one could only see a few humble peasants' houses rising gray and desolate against the golden glory of the setting sun. No trace of gorgeous temples, of thronged streets, of the mighty legions who started from this very spot to vanquish the Barbarians and to conquer new and immense lands for Rome.

No trace of the great Emperor's passage as, surrounded by his fantastic knights, he hunted the deer through the vast forests.

Nothing even of feudal times. The luxurious palace of the Patriarchs has disappeared, their armies gone, their treasure dispersed; only a few tombs remain in a silent and deserted church.

And yet, if energy and intelligence were to be expended in this abandoned spot where now the peasant drives his plough, a new world would rise in all the glory of white marble limbs—a new world, and yet so old! Shaking off the sleep of centuries from their solemn eyes, the gods and the nymphs, the heroes and the statesmen would live again, and once more Aquileia would rise from her ashes, the proud daughter of Imperial Rome.

The drive home in the cool of the evening—a wonderful soft June evening—was very pleasant. The air was heavy with sweet scents, the sun was setting in a crimson sky and flooding the green vineyards with golden rays, whilst the dark shadows grew longer and longer, and the blue mists veiled the distant hills. But our peaceful enjoyment

ENTRANCE TO CASTLE DUINO

was spoiled by the gloominess of "our host," who, having met a bicycle on the way, failed absolutely and entirely to recover his equanimity. He talked to us with great eloquence on the subject (bicycles are against his principles), but we gradually grew more and more sleepy, and only the view of the old castle rising dark against the paling sky (and the hope of our dinner) had the power to rouse our despondent and drooping spirits again.

CHAPTER VII

VILLA VICENTINA

> Gray twilight pour'd
> On dewy pastures, dewy trees,
> Softer than sleep—all things in
>   order stored,
> A haunt of ancient Peace.
>
>   TENNYSON.

My collaborator and I drove to Villa Vicentina on Friday, June 7th. We took a lady who is possessed with the photographic mania with us, thinking she might be useful, and the Other Boy to carry her camera, etc. There was no rising at unearthly hours in the morning this time—we started at a respectable hour in the afternoon. The early part of our drive was along the same road by which we went to Aquileia—the long white road bordered with poplars leading through the marshes. After passing through

Monfalcone and crossing the bridge over the Isonzo, however, we turned to the right. Hedges of acacia shadowed the road; the flowers are over, here, by June, but the leaves have still their first freshness, the beautiful tender green that the sun seems to love to illumine and brighten into golden yellow. We crossed a little river, a placid stream fringed with graceful willows and bordered with blue forget-me-nots, flowing through the level meadows and sweet-smelling vineyards, and at last came to the gate of Villa Vicentina. The house stands some distance from the road in a large park that, with its huge trees and rich grass, reminds one of dear old England. The trees are really magnificent, mostly white poplars ("the light quivering aspen"), venerable oaks, and towering sombre pines. We got out of our carriage, and walked part of the way to the house

> Mid mystic trees, where light falls in
> Hardly at all.

I like big trees, particularly on a hot day; it is so cool and pleasant under their green shade, where no sunlight comes but in little chequered patches here and there, when outside everything is bathed in the scorching rays, and you see the air tremulous with heat.

LITTLE RIVER NEAR VILLA VICENTINA

The Villa Vicentina formerly belonged to Princess Baciocchi, the sister of Napoleon I. Her daughter left it to the late Prince Imperial, and after his death it became the property of the Empress Eugénie. She never comes here—it is left in charge of an old

VILLA VICENTINA

caretaker and his wife, who, with another lady, possibly their daughter, and a female servant, appear to form the establishment. There is nothing particular about the house—it is an ordinary country villa. All the finer things have been taken away too, but there are still some bits of interesting furniture.

It was a strange feeling, not without a tinge of sadness, that stole over one whilst going up and down the deserted staircases and peeping into the empty rooms. Here and there a marble bust with the classic profile of the Buonapartes, an engraving, a faded water-colour, on the scanty remnants of furniture the Imperial eagle, some old firearms, the slender hand of beautiful Pauline Borghese cast in marble, a few bits of rare china, and everywhere the peculiar smell of damp and age that pervades long-unused houses. Where are the eagles now that once spread their wings over all Europe? Where are the famous beauties? Where are the glorious dreams?

But where are the snows of yester-year?

. . . . .

To be truthful, this last bit is not mine. My collaborator has just been worrying the life out of me to make me grow enthusiastic about Napoleon, but it is useless—quite useless. I am *not* enthusiastic about him, nor about his eagles, nor about his dreams. In fact, I cannot bear him, and he and Wagner make my life a burden. I do not admire them—I wish they had never existed. When those two unhappy beings are mentioned I know people will "jump on" me and abuse me. I bear it all as a martyr, but I absolutely cannot write with enthusiastic admiration about "old Nap" or stay in the room when there is Wagner music going on. So my collaborator has found it necessary to add these lines to my sketch. I do not call this fair, for when *I* write something *she* does not like, I have no rest till it is cut out. I know that some time or other Wagner will be brought in somehow, and I protest against it even now. It is a comfort that "our host" is of my opinion about Wagner. He says that he has lost all respect for him since he once went to see some Zulus that were exhibited somewhere, and found that those simple and unsophisticated savages with their war-music could make ever so much more noise than a whole orchestra playing Wagner. He says, too, that, after all, he only once went to a Wagner opera, and discovered that the unhappy tenor or baritone was obliged to make a whole shoe on the stage. No humbug, you know. He had to begin from the beginning and to make that whole shoe (a real serviceable article—no pretence about it) to perfection and to sing all the time till he had finished it. Our host could not stand it. He left the house to give the poor man a chance, and when he came back after two hours, there was the unhappy fellow still hammering away at his shoe, singing quite feebly, for he had no breath left in him. This time he went away for good, and never went to a Wagner opera again.

There! that has done me good.

. . . . .

The gardens are beautiful — nice old-fashioned gardens where one could wander about all day with pleasure. There is a pretty conservatory with some wonderful climbing geraniums. What delighted us most was a little walk about a hundred yards long, and quite straight, with a trellis-work covered with creepers—a perfect tunnel. At the farther end is an old stone table and seat, where we intended to have tea. It was a charming spot, but unfortunately we were almost devoured by mosquitoes—they seem to be particularly ferocious and bloodthirsty there. The lady-photographer took some photographs, but I am sorry to say *she* is an utter fraud. Generally there is nothing at all on the plate, and if there is, you are quite at a loss to know whether the photograph represents a landscape, a dog, or a flash of lightning.

We had brought a huge basket, like a Noah's ark, with us, which contained the "tea-things." My collaborator told me during the drive that they (the tea-things) had originally been packed in a much larger basket, but that she (with characteristic thoughtfulness) had taken them all out and repacked them again in this "small" one. Personally I had looked forward to tea all afternoon. It was very hot, and I was thirsty, so it was with feelings of joyous expectancy that I began unpacking the following articles :—

1. Two forks.
2. Some butter (in a liquid state) wrapped up in white paper.
3. The poems of Rossetti (neatly bound).
4. Three drawing pencils.
5. Two cups (without saucers).
6. A telescope.
7. Three tablets of Pears' soap (unscented).
8. A little bottle containing something—we didn't dare to open it. I fancy it was poison, and had some connection with photography.
9. A bottle of milk (sour).
10. Two enormous bottles of spirit of wine (to boil the kettle).
11. No kettle!
12. No tea!!

Happily the "Photographic Lady" (who considers tea a diabolical beverage) had some cake and some cherries mixed up with her apparatus, so, after all, our "tea" was rather a success— our tea on the old stone bench of Villa Vicentina, where the mosquitoes flourish!

There is a tree in the garden that was brought from the Emperor's grave in St. Helena. This is the end of the chapter. I finish it up quickly, or my collaborator will have a fit of enthusiasm again

CHAPTER VIII

AGRADO AND GRADISCA

> Blossoms of grape-vines scent the sunny air.
> LONGFELLOW.

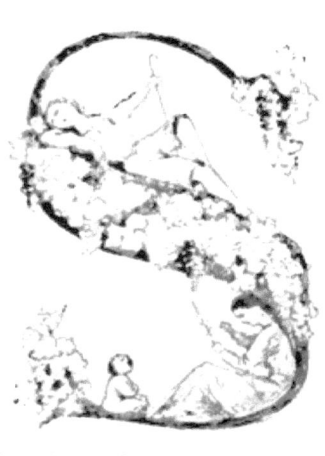

THE usual quartette went to Sagrado and Gradisca—two little Italian-like towns—on Saturday, 15th June.

There is one great drawback about Duino—there are only two roads. One goes to Trieste and the other doesn't. It is rather monotonous always driving along the same road. Familiarity breeds contempt, and even poplar-trees and marshes pall on one in time. However, "what can't be cured must be endured," and if you do not want to go to Trieste you must go the other way, even if it has grown almost too familiar. We branched off on a new road after passing through Monfalcone, and soon came to Sagrado. It is quite a little place, more of a village than a town, but there is an old villa standing in a large park, which was the attraction here. Two magnificent cypresses stand at the entrance-gate, one on each side, and the park is beautiful, full of fine trees, especially oaks overgrown with ivy. It forms a great contrast to the surrounding country, which towards Duino is barren and stony in the extreme. One has a magnificent view from the villa. It stands on a hill, and the valley of the Isonzo stretches below it. Far on the left one catches a glimpse of the sea. Before one, far as the eye can reach, is the plain, covered with vineyards, like waves of a billowy sea of emerald green, with tiny villages nestling here and there (the "Photographic Lady" says you can count two thousand of them, but I am afraid some untruthful person has imposed on her credulity), and the blue river winding through it, like some giant snake; and on the right, rising higher and higher as they fade away into the shadowy distance, are the snow-capped Alps.

The house is an old villa of the Italian style, with stuccoed walls, and on the floor the pretty Italian "terrazzi." In the hall, just when you enter, one is struck by four quaint old pictures of four men almost life-size; they are dressed in the peasant's costume of the country, of last century, and each holds a little money-bag in his hand. It seems that these worthy people were four farmers, who, when a former owner of the property (one of the Della Torre) was in financial difficulties and on the verge of ruin, came forward and paid off his debts. In gratitude to them he had their portraits painted and put in his entrance-hall. What a pity it is that people don't do this sort of thing nowadays! If any one feels inclined to follow the example of the four farmers and pay off *my* debts, I will faithfully promise to have his photograph taken and placed on my writing-table. I am only sorry I cannot rise to oil-paintings and entrance-halls.

From the pretty marble staircase you enter a charming drawing-room in the Italian Louis XVI. style. The walls are green marmorino, with ornaments of white stucco, and big mirrors let into them. There is a very large dining-hall of great height, with its walls and ceiling painted in fresco. No one lives in the villa at present.

The gardens must have been very pretty—all terraces and staircases—when they were kept in the style of the time. They are rather neglected now, and seem to be only inhabited by a perfect army of nightingales. A queer little red house is at the farther end of the garden, with a crypt under it and an imitation tomb. The walls are covered with mottoes—Greek, Latin, French, etc., and there is one in English : " Happiness is of a retired nature, and an enemy of pomp and noise." The individual who built the house must have been very much struck by this last motto, for it seems that he used to live in this little dismal-looking place all alone, in the one room over the crypt, leaving his smiling villa untenanted at the top of the hill.

We had tea in the park. It is a great mistake to wander about to find a suitable spot for tea—you are sure to pick out the worst possible place. It is much better to stop under the first shady tree one comes to, and to sit down there. On this occasion the ladies chose the situation, and when tea was about half over we found we were sitting on an ant-heap. It was hardly worth moving then, though, so we stayed where we were, and pretended to be very much interested in the movements of the ants. I made the tea. I have a way of my own for making it, which is, I believe, sometimes practised by homeless wanderers in foreign countries--it is very superior to civilised methods. I am not selfish, and I have not taken out a patent for it, so I have no objection to presenting my method to the world, free, gratis, and for nothing. This is my recipe. Boil the water in the kettle, and when fiercely boiling put in your tea (one teaspoonful for each person and one for the kettle) and stir up the mixture. Let it go on boiling for a few seconds, and then pour out and drink. You will find you have excellent tea in this way. *N.B.*—It is as well to have a strainer with you to get rid of the tea-leaves.

My collaborator had often stayed at the villa as a child, and had hosts of acquaintances. I was interested to know who the various ladies and gentlemen who kept addressing her were, but her explanations were so confusing that I soon gave up inquiring. I remember that one lady was " the sister-in-law of a gardener, who was the step-brother of a cousin of the late wife of the man with the wig, who was the old butler." I cannot grasp such involved relationships —they are too much for *my* intellect. I made the acquaintance of the " man with the wig " afterwards. We called to ask him to order supper to be ready for us at the little inn when we came back from Gradisca. Then we drove on to Gradisca. You cross the Isonzo to get there, and there is a lovely view from the bridge, of the blue river and the distant Alps. Gradisca is a nice little old-fashioned town. The inhabitants are evidently not accustomed to visitors, and we caused an immense sensation. The "Photographic Lady" took several photographs, and she was always the centre of an admiring crowd. They were rather disappointed, I fancy, not to see any

PALAZZO FINETTI

results then and there. They caused the lady great annoyance by going and standing before the camera to get a better view of the performance—in fact, she got quite angry, and abused them in all the four languages of the country.

There is a fine old palace in Gradisca that once belonged to the Della Torre. The whole of this part of the country seems to have belonged to them, and

HOUSE AT GRADISCA

everywhere—in churches, on old houses, over doors —you see the tower with crossed lilies that was their coat of arms. In this particular house I was struck by a charming courtyard with graceful "loggia" and a flight of steps from both sides to the ground.

We went to see two churches. The first contained nothing interesting, but the second is worth seeing. There is a tomb there erected to the memory of Nicolao Della Torre in a private burial-chapel.

TOMB OF NICOLAO DELLA TORRE

The monument is very large, with a recumbent figure of the gentleman lying in full armour. He must have been of unusual size, with a fine regular face and a long flowing beard, and is very much like the portraits of Martin the Giant. He, too, fought against the infidels, being General of the

Imperial troops that protected the Hungarian frontier against the Turks. He was badly wounded in one of the battles, but his end was not so tragic as that of his ancestor, and he now lies peacefully in the little church of Gradisca, enjoying at last the strange old motto of his family—" Tranquillité."

The stuccoed ceiling of the chapel, which seems to be particularly fine, was pointed out to me, but somehow I had had too much of churches and monuments for one day, so I was not so appreciative as I suppose I ought to have been. In any case, I was again the victim of sundry abuse.

After all this sight-seeing it was a pleasure to wander quietly and aimlessly through the quaint little streets, meeting only an occasional donkey or dirty baby, who stared very much, whilst at the windows one would sometimes catch a glimpse of a pair of big black eyes following one curiously from behind a row of red carnations. We admired the old walls of the town, which was strongly fortified in ancient times—enormous black walls with battlements, and beneath them a sort of green lawn shadowed by numerous chestnut-trees, the fashionable promenade of the high life of Gradisca.

We drove back to Sagrado and had supper in the little inn. The " man with the wig " waited on us with a beaming face. I did not feel at all happy, for we had the most horrid wine it has ever been my lot to drink. It is the wine of the country, and said to be the pure juice of the grape (everything nasty seems to be "the pure juice of the grape"). One drinks it diluted with water, and it has a most extraordinary bitter taste. The ladies assured me that I should soon grow accustomed to it, and then I should never like any other wine as well. I had my own opinion on the subject, but I had to smile and look pleasant.

We drove home in the evening. I had foretold a thunderstorm all the afternoon, but had been laughed to scorn by everybody. My prophecies were correct, however, for we had hardly left Sagrado when the storm began. I never saw more vivid lightning—the whole sky was lighted up by it, and it was almost incessant. The weird effect was increased, too, by the fireflies—there must have been millions of them flitting hither and thither, like the lost souls of the departed. We had a great argument as to whether we should remain at Monfalcone till the storm had passed over. The ladies were in favour of waiting, the coachman and I were for going on, and the boy was neutral, being fast asleep. Our eloquence prevailed—we hurried on. It was a desperate race, but we had the satisfaction of beating the worst of the storm by some ten seconds.

After all, I did not think much of Sagrado and Gradisca, and I can only say I hope people will be as bored in reading this chapter as I have been in writing it.

CHAPTER IX

 GHOSTS

> All houses wherein men have lived and died
>   Are haunted houses. Through the open
>   doors
> The harmless phantoms on their errands glide,
>   With feet that make no sound upon the
>   floors.
>
> We meet them at the doorway, on the stair,
>   Along the passages they come and go,
> Impalpable impressions on the air,
>   A sense of something moving to and fro.
>
> There are more guests at table than the hosts
>   Invited ; the illuminated hall
> Is thronged with quiet, inoffensive ghosts,
>   As silent as the pictures on the wall.
>
>   LONGFELLOW.

GHOSTS! There is a charm in the very word. Tales of gruesome apparitions told over a blazing fire at Christmas-time come back to one—tales told long years ago, when, after hearing them, one was almost afraid to go to bed ; when one started at every shadow on the stairs and imagined it was some dark denizen of the spirit world come to carry us off; when, being fairly in bed and the light out, we drew the sheets over our heads to shut out the phantoms that appeared in the darkness.

From my earliest childhood I was always a firm believer in ghosts—the good old-fashioned ghost, I mean,—the unhappy lady or gentleman who appears at twelve o'clock at night with wailings and groans, and rattles chains and carries his or her head under his or her arm. That is the sort of ghost *I* like.

I have a contempt for the feeble ghost of to-day the spirit that raps on tables and moves chairs, that writes letters backwards that no one can read, and never shows itself or behaves in a rational manner. The modern ghost is very degenerate.

My collaborator is a member of the Society for Psychical Research, so I must be careful what I say, or I shall be abused again. We had a grand *séance* on the evening of 16th June. It was held in the "Emperor's Room"—so called because the Emperor Leopold I. is said to have slept there. His portrait is painted on the ceiling, which, by the way, is of wonderful Venetian stucco, with cupids and garlands of fruits and flowers all over it. It is a haunted room. It is not the Emperor that appears here,

however, but a much more interesting sort of person—
the White Lady. She had a cruel husband who threw

THE WHITE LADY

her down the cliff under the ruin. Her body may
still be seen, as she was turned into stone, a gigantic
woman wrapped in a long white garment—ever-

lastingly climbing up the cliff, but never getting any higher. Her spirit returns to the castle and

THE WHITE LADY

searches for her lost children. On nights when the moon is full one can hear the rustling of her robes, as she wanders disconsolately about in the "Emperor's Room."

We carried out our *séance* on the most approved methods. Eight of us—my collaborator, the Energetic Lady, the Photographic Lady, Miss Umslopogaas, the two learned men, the Seal, and myself—sat round a little oval table with both our hands on it, and clasped each other's little fingers. The learned Dark Man calculated that there were eighty fingers on that table. "Better eighty fingers on one table than eighty tables on one finger" remarked our host. He was rather a nuisance (our host, I mean), as he insisted on walking about the room and smoking cigarettes. He also kept turning up the lamp (ghosts dislike much light, and it is necessary to respect their feelings) to see how we were getting on.

There was also a dog in the room. This dog rejoices in the name of "Tin-ho"—he is a Chinese animal. I believe he is the last of his race, or something of that sort, and is the most cherished possession of the Energetic Lady. He is one of the banes of my life—he, Napoleon I., and Wagner. I like animals—in fact, I love them—especially cats and dogs. But *this* dog is too much for me. I have made the most friendly overtures to him. I have called him by the most endearing terms. I have even learned some

Italian (he only understands that language) especially for his benefit, and have said *poverissima bellissima* to him with a pathos that would have moved a stone

TIN-HO — FIRST-CLASS MANDARIN

statue to tears. But it is of no use. He is as unfriendly as ever, and treats me with contempt. Now I kick him, whenever the Energetic Lady is not anywhere near him, which is not very often, by the way.

I have not explained yet who Miss Umslopogaas is. She is a lady who is staying here, and her proper name is difficult to pronounce — at least, I cannot conquer it. I began by calling her Miss Asparagus, but that sounds too much like a vegetable, and is familiar besides. Umslopogaas is quite as much like what I can imagine her real name to be, and has the advantage of sounding more foreign.

Well, we sat round that table for an hour and a half. My collaborator was delighted at the beginning—she was sure the Seal was a perfect medium, as he trembled all over and felt cold. (I have my own private opinion about it.) The table, too, moved occasionally (no wonder, when the Seal was shaking like an aspen leaf), so she was convinced something was about to happen.

At last something did happen!

An unearthly shriek rang through the haunted chamber. There was a sound of scuffling and struggling, a smothered exclamation.

The Photographic Lady leaped a foot from her chair and showed a tendency to go into hysterics. The Seal's teeth chattered with fright.

But, after all, it was only our host who had trodden on the dog.

We sat on. The Photographic Lady flirted with

the learned Fair Man, and Miss Umslopogaas pinched the little finger of the learned Dark Man; but no ghost appeared. I think there were too many of us, or we were not serious enough, or the vagaries of our host and the dog were too much for the spirits. But, in any case, our *séance* was a failure, and we had no manifestations at all.

We gave it up then, and took to telling ghost-stories. The Photographic Lady related an experience of her own. Some three or four years ago she went into the great banqueting hall in the evening, and there saw the figure of a man. He was of immense height, elderly, and with a long flowing beard, and his face was vividly impressed on her memory. He advanced towards her, and then suddenly disappeared. According to her own account she was not at all frightened. At the time she did not know who it was, but on visiting the church at Gradisca some time later, she recognised the ghost at once as the Della Torre who is carved in stone on the tomb there, an ancestor of her own.

The Energetic Lady had had a strange experience in the same room. She was there alone, and a *chair* began to move about of its own accord. It moved forwards—it moved backwards—it moved sideways, and then in a slow and stately manner it waltzed round and round. With her usual energy, she chased it, caught it, *sat down* on it, but it continued its antics, she still sitting on it. She said it was an uncomfortable sensation and confessed to feelings of alarm—in fact, she left the apartment in haste.

At this point the Seal said he should retire, as he did not like to talk of such things. Miss Umslopogaas also took her departure—she did not consider ghosts quite proper. She thought they should not appear in people's bedrooms uninvited. Some of them were so insufficiently clothed too!

The two learned men disputed on ghosts generally. They had different theories on the matter.

My collaborator listened with a look of supreme contempt. She does not care to relate *her* experiences to the common herd. I was so crushed by her superior manner that I was too modest to tell any story. I never saw a ghost myself, but an intimate friend of mine has had that pleasure.

Our host was not bashful, however. This is what *he* said: "I like ghosts, because they never come. If there are ten persons in a room, eight are fools, one is a rascal, the tenth might be all right . . . but *he* is generally dead. I have no objection to *his* coming. Still, as 'Happiness is of a retired nature,' I think him very considerate never to do so."

I did not see any point in this, but every one else seemed to find it very amusing.

Suddenly the great clock in the tower began striking—slowly—twelve!

Then we all went to bed.

.   .   .   .   .

We are all haunted by ghosts—ghosts of old friends, old scenes. We sit alone, and the past rises up before us. They are all with us again—the friends of our childhood, of our school-days, of our "Varsity" life. Once more we feel the warm clasp of their hands, once more we hear the merry voices and look into the kindly faces we knew long years ago.

Picture follows picture.

We see the old garden where we played as children, our brothers and sisters, our child-friends, the old house, the flowers, the green lawn. It is all so familiar, and yet it was all so long ago.

The scene changes: a long, low room, desks hacked with pocket-knives and stained with ink, a hot, drowsy afternoon, a hum of voices, the master's desk, the master himself in cap and gown, a crowd of boys.

The scene changes again. Stately buildings appear before us, old courts and cloisters, the gleam of the river. Old familiar sounds ring in our ears: the thud of the oars in the rowlocks, the click of the cricket-bat, the tramp of feet on the football field.

Fair faces pass before us too. We hear the rustle of their dresses, their girlish laughter, their soft voices, we see the bright eyes that look into ours, the rosy lips that murmured words we shall never forget.

> There are things of which I may not speak;
>   There are dreams that cannot die!
> There are thoughts that make the strong heart weak,
> And bring a pallor into the cheek,
>   And a mist before the eye.
>   And a verse of a sweet old song
>   Is haunting my memory still:
>   A boy's will is the wind's will,
> And the thoughts of youth are long, long thoughts.

Where are they all — those friends of other days?

Gone — some dead — all scattered; we have lost sight of most of them. Some are sleeping on distant battlefields or beneath the waves of the hungry sea, some are preaching their message of peace in busy town or quiet village, some fighting with disease and death in the crowded hospitals of great cities, some working their way upwards through dusty law-courts or in foreign lands. But here — in Shadow-Land — they one and all come back to us.

CHAPTER X

APODISTRIA

Happy star reign now !
Here comes Bohemia.
SHAKESPEARE
(*The Winter's Tale*).

THIS chapter is remarkable, since it introduces a new and interesting character to the public, to wit the "Gentle Lunatic," who rushed down upon us from the wild and boundless forests of Bohemia.

We journeyed to Capodistria on Saturday, 22nd June, the "Gentle One" filling the place of the "Other Boy" in the usual quartette.

We left Duino at 8 o'clock in the morning (another early start), and drove to Nabresina; from thence we went to Trieste by train. Our train was half an hour late, for which we abused the

"Photographic Lady," as she had made all the arrangements for the journey.

It is marvellous how our arrangements always go wrong! We have tried all the ladies in turn as superintendent-in-chief: the "Energetic One," who did not want any railway guide or any advice, but knew everything generally; the "Photographic Lady," who smothered herself and everybody else with books, time-tables, etc., asked every one's opinion collectively and singly, and made an elaborate plan beforehand; my collaborator, who did not care a rap how things went, supposed they would be sure to come right somehow, and when they did *not*, said it was destiny; but none of them answered. We were always in a hopeless muddle, either starting too soon, or too late, or not at all.

We were very much annoyed by the dilatory conduct of our train, even when it arrived at Nabresina. It is extraordinary the length of time it takes to start a continental train! A bell rings violently and then tolls *one*. This is to inform the passengers that the train is in the station. A long interval follows. The bell rings more violently than before and then tolls *two*. This shows that in the course of time the train will proceed. There is no hurry, however. You have plenty of time still to make a substantial meal and pay calls on any friends you may have in the neighbourhood of the station. The bell rings a third time and tolls *three*. The conductor suggests the advisability of taking your seat, the engine-driver and stoker go for their last drink, and the stationmaster begins to play with a little horn he wears suspended round his neck. The conductors—there are generally two or three of them on each train—having ascertained that none of the passengers have any particular wish to remain any longer, step out upon the platform, shout *ready*, and blow whistles. The stationmaster, with an air of immense importance, sounds his toy trumpet, the engine utters a scream of defiance to the world generally, and after a decent interval, to avoid the semblance of haste, the train crawls out of the station. It is an imposing ceremony, but as it is repeated at every small station on the line, it grows somewhat monotonous and makes railway-travelling rather a formidable and lengthy business. At last, however, our train, having rested sufficiently, proceeded slowly on its journey, and we arrived in the course of time at Trieste.

We drove to the Hotel Delorme, and ordered lunch to be ready in an hour. The "Gentle Lunatic" announced his intention of going to find some tame turtles. He said he meant to buy a dozen, and we could take them home in our pockets. He could dispose of six, and we three should have two each. We argued and remonstrated, but it was of no use—he went.

Meanwhile the two ladies and I set out to see the Church of St. Just, a very fine church—in fact, one of the oldest Christian basilicae. It is a great pity that the beautiful old columns are covered with red damask. They look like a forest of pillars, and divide the church into five aisles. Two of the many altars are bright with very ancient Byzantine gold-grounded mosaics.

The " Photographic Lady " took a photograph of the interior and carried on a flirtation with a young verger, to whom she promised a photograph, whether of herself or the church we were unable to discover. We were then joined by the " Gentle One," who was quite heart-broken, as he had not been able to find his turtles.

Trieste is a nice town. It is a pity it is not a pleasure resort instead of a mercantile place, as it is beautifully situated on green hills sloping quite gently down to the sea; the surroundings are pretty, and brightened with villas and flower-covered cottages.

We went on to Capodistria by steamer. There

was a very motley crowd of passengers on board—
peasants returning from market, business people
bound for an afternoon's pleasure-seeking, persons
of all sorts and conditions. The "Photographic
Lady" was delighted that, in one particular at least,
her researches with regard to our arrangements were
correct—namely, that the steamer had left Trieste at
one o'clock. To prove her accuracy, she asked the
"G. L." soon after starting to tell her the time.
But his answer was somewhat vague, and his method
of ascertaining the time appeared to us peculiar.
He took out his watch, looked at it for a long time,
gazed fixedly at the sun, shut his eyes, seemed by
the contortion of his features to be going through
some abstruse calculation, and then said it was
between one and two o'clock. This nettled the lady,
and she replied rather warmly that she wanted to
know the *exact time*. With a mournful smile he
took out his watch again, went through the previous
programme, and gave the same answer. At this we
all insisted on seeing his watch for ourselves, and
then the mystery was explained. It had no glass!
it had no hands! We suggested that such a watch
must be rather inconvenient, but he assured us it
was the best watch he had ever had in his life; for
more than ten years it had been in this state, during

which time it had gone absolutely perfectly, and had never needed the slightest attention beyond winding up.

It took us three-quarters of an hour to reach Capodistria. It looks very quaint and old-fashioned this little out-of-the-way town, with its red-roofed houses, blue sky above, and blue sea all around, and the great gaunt prison lighted up by the golden rays of the sun, and forming a bright patch of yellow in the landscape. My collaborator says the prison spoils the appearance of the town, but I maintain that it forms a pleasing contrast to the old gray walls of the houses.

Capodistria was formerly Byzantine, but in 1278 it became Venetian. Under the Republic of Venice it was a very flourishing place, and is said to have been the richest town in Istria. There were many wealthy patrician families, renowned for their luxurious living, inhabiting it. With the fall of the Venetian Republic, Capodistria declined, and it is now a small unimportant town. It was formerly known by the name of " the Gentlewoman of Istria."

On arriving, we found that we had made a mistake of two hours in the time of the return steamer, a discovery that threw all our plans out of gear, but we comforted ourselves with the reflection that it gave us more time to see the place. We engaged a chariot and drove off to inspect the town. It was a remarkable conveyance. The "G. L." selected it, and it appeared as if he had chosen the dirtiest he could find. It was small too. We could only just squeeze in, and were very much cramped for room; but any trifling defects in the carriage were amply made up for by the horse. This was indeed a noble animal, and high spirited in the extreme; the driver too was perfectly reckless, so we dashed off at the rate of some sixty miles an hour, the chariot pitching and tossing like a small boat in an angry sea.

The "piazza" is quite the sight of Capodistria, and is very picturesque. A church stands on one side of it, and before one is an old Town Hall, turreted on both sides, with graceful Venetian windows, innumerable inscriptions, coats-of-arms, and other carvings, and the whole crowned by the Venetian lion. A pretty outer staircase with little marble columns runs along part of the front of the building, and under it there is a deep and sombre archway, through which one sees a narrow street, with great, high, irregularly built houses almost meeting above it.

I believe we went to see three churches in this little town, but I have seen such a superabundance of churches lately, that I cannot remember the

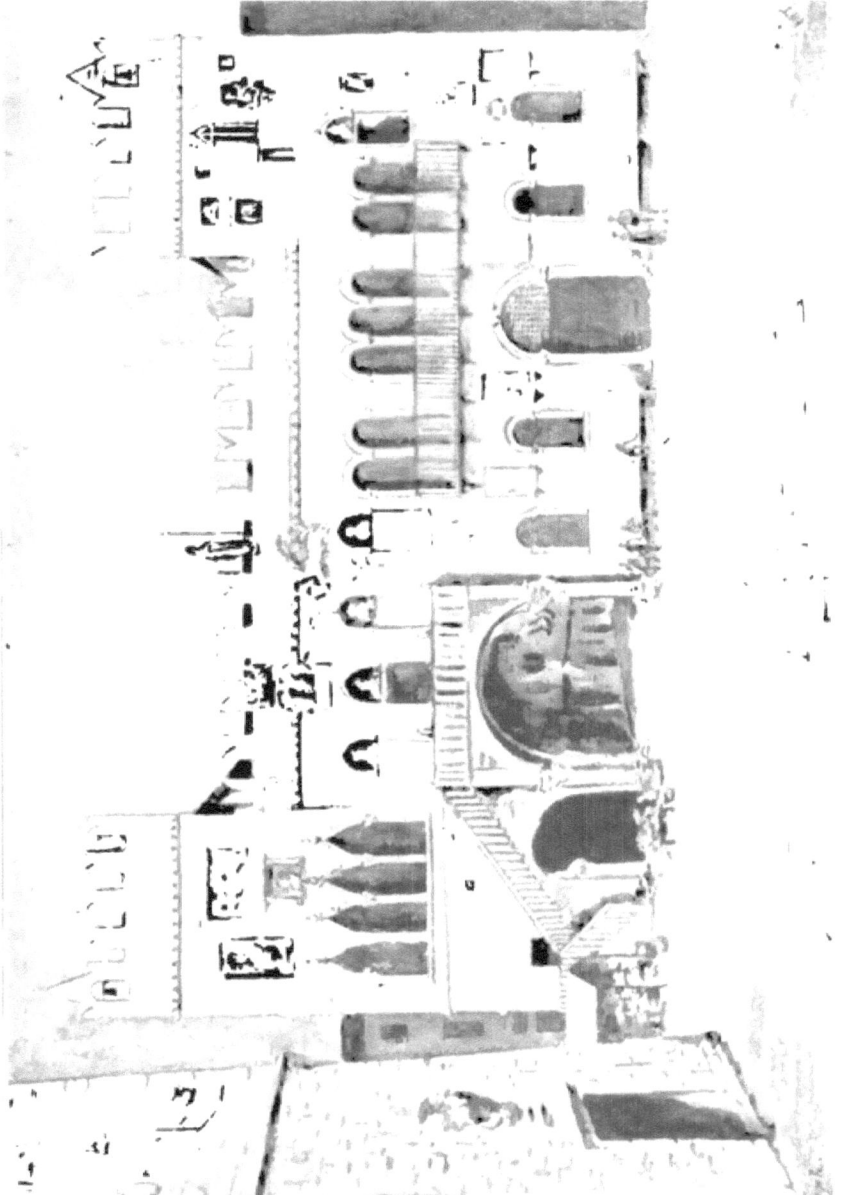

THE TOWN HALL

characteristic features of any of the three. I know that in one there was a quantity of fine old silver, and that we were shown round another by a most obsequious monk, clad in russet brown, who explained its beauties to us in a confidential manner. I remember, too, that we saw some pictures. In one church (the "G. L." says it was in the big one on the piazza) there was a very fine one of Benedetto Carpaccio—the Madonna in the company of some saints, and with two little angels playing the banjo (it may be a guitar) at her feet. In the church where we interviewed the monk there was a big altar-piece of Cima da Conegliano, very much spoilt by having been restored, and a most curious picture of Vittore Carpaccio, with a garland of angels' heads (hundreds of them), some painted in natural colours and some bright *red*. (Red-headed angels—this is art !)

By the way, I was told that in Venice there is a very old picture attributed to the same Carpaccio, and said to represent the Lords of Duino taking tribute from the town of Zara ; the Lords of Duino, in quaint armour, with their ladies and soldiers, on the one side of the picture ; on the other, the representatives of the vanquished town bringing gold, etc., and in the background a turreted castle—Duino, and a town near it—Trieste. As Carpaccio was a native of Capodistria, it is very probable that he painted this triumph of some of the most powerful barons of his country.

After this came more sight-seeing. We visited a funny old drinking-fountain known as the "Bridge" (why, I know not), and watched the women drawing water.

It is a sleepy and dull little town, with small streets and dark forbidding-looking houses. There are hardly any shops, but in one quaint sort of jeweller's stall the fashionable ornaments of Istria were pointed out to me. These are ear-rings—little crowned negroes' heads in black and white enamel, and the height of fashion among the fishermen is to wear both in one ear.

One sees very few people in the streets. Here and there a dark-eyed girl strolling along with the peculiar shuffling gait caused by the "zoccoli"— the wooden slippers of the Venetian women.

Everywhere are relics of Venice — the carved cisterns on the piazzas, the winged lions on the houses, where you find inscriptions bearing some of the most illustrious names of the Republic, but everywhere, too, silence, abandonment, and decay. There are some fine old palaces, but the windows are shut, and they seem deserted. On one we admired a wonderful old bronze knocker of most refined workman-

DOOR-KNOCKER

ship, and as the house with its arched windows and marble balconies looked particularly nice, we explored the interior. There, too, we found the large Venetian entrance-hall and an imposing-looking staircase, but no soul appeared.

Then we repaired to a *café* on the piazza. It was formerly an open "loggia," but between the stately marble columns some mean commercial soul

CAFÉ AT CAPODISTRIA

has put glass windows, and the interior is dishonoured by the usual little marble tables and black leather seats. The ladies ordered coffee and sponge-cakes, I drank beer, and the "Gentle Lunatic" asked for a cup of hot water—his favourite drink.

One of the "G. L.'s" passions is his liking for

low acquaintances. Hardly had we finished our repast and gone out, before he formed a new friendship of this kind. An old beggar with a long gray beard approached, and the two immediately fraternised. They sat down on a stone bench together, and discussed politics and literature. In the meantime another beggar came up, whom the first beggar introduced as "the greatest poet of Capodistria." The poet was proud, however, and evidently averse to becoming intimate with strangers; at any rate, after having received with lofty condescension the "tip" diffidently offered to him by the "G. L.," he went majestically off. It was with the greatest difficulty that we finally separated the two friends, who parted with mutual expressions of everlasting esteem.

We then once more mounted our chariot, and betook ourselves to the steamer.

So good-bye to "the Gentlewoman of Istria," lying placidly asleep by the blue waters of the Adriatic. Though changed and abandoned, you can still distinguish some of the charms that won for her that poetic name. May she dream of the glorious time long ago—the glorious time of her youth, when she was growing and blooming in the shade of the mighty wings that Saint Mark's lion was once spreading over land and sea!

CHAPTER XI

GORITZ

> In the greenest of our valleys.
>
> E. A. POE.

On Monday, 24th June, we went to Goritz — my collaborator, the "Gentle Lunatic," and I. Our party had already broken up — the "Energetic Lady" and the "Seal," Miss Umslopogaas, the two learned men, the Thin Boy, the Other Boy, even "our host" — all had gone. And now we left too. My collaborator was going on to Venice from Goritz, and the G. L. and I, after picking up the Fat Boy at Nabresina, were going to Vienna by the night train.

We drove to Monfalcone, and then went on by rail.

Goritz is charmingly situated in the smiling valley of the Isonzo. I have spoken of the beauty of this valley before, but never does it strike one so pleasantly as when one approaches Goritz. It is a forest of vineyards surrounded by tier upon tier of majestic mountains, that rise higher and higher, until they are lost to sight among the clouds, and in the centre of the mass of greenery, on the banks of the blue river, nestles the little town.

Not much is known of the early history of Goritz. From the twelfth century, however, it seems to have played an important part in the history of the country, and the Counts of Goritz stand out prominently as a powerful and warlike family, second in importance only to the Patriarchs of Aquileia. They were celebrated for their munificence and for the splendour of the tournaments promoted by them. By the way, an old chronicle says that in 1224 a great tournament, arranged by Mainardo II., Count of Goritz, was held at Trieste. To this came Ulrich of Lichtenstein, the German Minnesänger, who always went about dressed as Venus. Unfortunately the details of his dress are wanting.

After the extinction of the family, Goritz came into the possession of the Emperors. The Venetians attempted to conquer it, and indeed appear to have held it for a short time. The town seems to have kept up its reputation of gaiety, as later chronicles speak of the lavish hospitality of the nobility residing there.

It is now quite a lively little place, with broad streets and good shops, and its outskirts are one charming garden full of pretty villas. There is not much to be seen in the way of antiquities—an old castle, by no means beautiful, perched on a hill, and some churches.

It was a very hot day. It is all very well to talk poetically of the sunny South, but for my part I wish it was not so confoundedly warm. We were taken to an antiquary's shop by my collaborator, and spent most of the morning there—she in looking over the things in a business-like manner, the G. L. in wandering aimlessly around, and I in sitting on the back stairs. (I found it the coolest place.)

We lunched with Count and Countess C., and, to speak truly, my pleasantest recollections of Goritz are associated with that lunch. I must say I had spent rather a miserable sort of morning, what with the heat and the antiquary's shop, but these troubles were soon forgotten on our arriving at their house.

It is an old-fashioned, rambling house, with low, dim rooms, furnished with a charming disregard to all pretence at style—old carved furniture side by side with little modern round tables, and valuable paintings of the last century hanging by oleographs of to-day. Every room, too, is a menagerie—dogs, cats, monkeys, snakes, birds of all sorts, are everywhere. I like a house of this kind—there is an entire absence of that bugbear *Art* (art with a big capital " A," you know), and most charming of all are its inhabitants. They are brother and sister, and both on the verge of eighty, the Countess the personification of goodness and the Lady Bountiful of the town, and the Count a curious mixture of the beau of the beginning of the century, poet, artist, and philosopher rolled into one. In spite of their age they both look marvellously young, and are more gay and active than the majority of young people I know.

We ate our lunch—which was excellent, by the way—in a little cool room that opens into the garden. The latter is as quaint as the house—roses and red currants grow together in luxuriant profusion. There is a delightful little arbour overgrown with white jasmine, and an old flight of steps that leads up to what was probably once a fortification, but is now a fine bed of cabbages with a border of hollyhocks, and the whole overshadowed by an enormous cherry-tree. Just outside the garden rises a big modern building, and from this, every now and then, a chorus of sweet girlish voices floated forth upon the still summer air. They were factory girls spinning silk, I was told, and singing over their work.

After lunch we adjourned to the Count's study—the most remarkable room in the house perhaps. It is lower than the street, very large and vaulted, full of old furniture and curiosities of every kind; here

A CAST

and there casts of famous sculptures, very white against the dark walls; on the many tables a litter of books and papers, except on one, where we were told to admire a collection of paper-knives.

It is an extraordinary thing that passion for collections. I knew a man once who collected *pipes*. He had one hundred and sixty-three when I saw him last, and he had stolen them all. I have no sympathy with this sort of thing, and quite disapproved of his actions—in fact, I withdrew from his acquaintance. I have too much affection for my own pipes to know such people. The "Gentle One" told me that a friend of his collected *old hats*. He labelled each hat with the name of its former owner, and studied his character from his head-covering. He knew a family too who collected buttons. They were accustomed to secretly steal them from their visitors' overcoats, with a view to scientifical and psychological research—of course!

Now I collect money. Do not think me a miser. I do not hoard it up—I spend it. I shall be delighted to receive help with my collection. I have no false pride—any contribution, however small, will be thankfully received, and acknowledged by return of post.

In the afternoon the "Gentle Lunatic" and I drove round to inspect the place. We made a sort of grand tour of the town, and then went out to a little village from which there is a view. It is a lovely view, too. You stand on a hill and look down into a valley, or rather glen; far below one flows the Isonzo, bluer than any sea or any sky, winding along, with a little cascade here and there, between banks thickly covered with oak woods, whilst above everything tower the mountains. Another interesting place near Goritz is the church and convent of Castagnavizza, not on account of the buildings, which are nothing remarkable, but because the last princes of the French Royal Family are buried there. They all lie in a little chapel (a Della Torre burial-ground, by the way), in simple coffins — Charles X. and his sons, the unfortunate Duchess of Angoulême, and, last of all, the Count and Countess of Chambord. It is a very gloomy vault, and one cannot help thinking of all the splendour and glory of Versailles, of all the memories of that long lineage of kings, and contrasting them with this their last resting-place, so humble and forsaken in a strange land—the royal lilies withered in a foreign soil.

After this visit one is glad to get out into the sunshine again and to ramble through the streets of the gay little town.

There are four languages generally spoken in Goritz—Italian, Slav, Friulan, and German. Friulan is an extraordinary language, a sort of Italian dialect.

only spoken in the Friul, as the neighbourhood of Goritz is called. German is, of course, the State language, but Italian is universally spoken all over the Littoral. The lower classes do not understand a word of German, and I have found that hardly any one understands *my* German. I had a forcible illustration of this not long ago. I was lunching with the Gentle Lunatic at a hotel, when an acquaintance of his came in and sat at our table. With my accustomed modesty, I said little or nothing until the G. L. suggested that I might air some of my German. I promptly opened conversation with a sentence I had learned from an exercise book—" The dog is more faithful than the cat." It was perhaps not the sort of remark one would as a rule make to a stranger, but I thought he would in all probability agree with my sentiments, and then it was one of the few complete German sentences I knew. The reply, however, was not what I expected. Instead of answering, " Yes, but have you seen the penknife of my grandmother's female gardener?" or something of that sort, he turned to the Gentle One—" Tell him," he said, " I am very sorry, but I have forgotten all my English." It was a crushing blow—he had mistaken my best German sentence for English!

The people of the Littoral are of the Italian type.

Many of the women are very handsome, and they have almost all fine eyes, large and black, and soft and velvety-looking. They hold themselves very well too, probably from being accustomed to carry baskets and bundles on their heads. Only the

GIRL FROM DUINO

better class women wear hats. The peasants wear nothing but their own luxuriant hair, or merely a coloured kerchief thrown gracefully over their heads. The height of fashion at present is a black kerchief with large red spots. The people generally are a good-natured, cheerful race. "They are dirty, they are rough and ready, but they have the heart in the right place," as the G. L.'s English butler says, and his words exactly describe them.

We stopped at an open-air *café* in driving back

CASTLE DUINO FROM THE RAILWAY

and drank some beer, and then we returned to Count C.'s and ate ices. Beer and ices are *not* a nice mixture. Don't try it if you have not already done so.

We saw my collaborator off, and then started ourselves for Vienna. The railway line runs quite close to Duino, so we had one more glimpse of the old castle from the train. There had been a thunder-storm in the afternoon, and the sky was still covered with black clouds. The sea was leaden-coloured and the far horizon blotted out by thick gray mist and rain streaks, but as we flattened our noses against the window-pane to "take a last fond look," one bright ray from the setting sun shone through the darkness of the thunder-clouds. It brightened the old gray walls of the castle, and bathed them in rosy light; it lingered lovingly round the great Roman tower, and lit up the red and white Hohenlohe banner that floated in the breeze.

And so I saw Duino for the last time.

CHAPTER XII

 OR NOTHING AT ALL

> Story! God bless you! I have none to tell, sir.

My collaborator is to blame for this chapter. She found that when the eleven chapters already written and the Introduction and the Conclusion (reckoning the two last as chapters) were added together, the result would be thirteen. And so I am to write one more, and there is nothing to write about. I feel myself to be a martyr offered up on the altar of superstition.

Superstition is all very well, but I think it can be carried too far. I was a victim to this fatal number 13 only the other day. I came in to lunch rather late, and was just going to sit down, when the "Energetic Lady" jumped up from the table with a howl of despair, taking her plate with her, and began to eat at a sideboard. She had seen that when I sat down there would be thirteen at table. Of course, I could not allow *her* to be made uncomfortable, so the result was that I had to go and sit at a little table by myself, and eat my lunch in lonely misery. I have known people too (I will not mention names) who would not start on a journey, or arrive at a place—in fact, I believe they absolutely do nothing—on the thirteenth of the month. I am rather superstitious myself about some things. I confess I always throw three grains of salt over my left shoulder if I should by any chance spill some; also I always tap my first and fourth fingers on something wooden, and say "unberufen" when I have made some such remark as "I have not had toothache for more than three years"; and then I invariably take off my hat to a single magpie. But then you cannot call these things superstitions—they are merely the force of habit.

"For use almost can change the stamp of nature," as Shakespeare says.

Speaking of superstitions reminds me that I have

known people who believe implicitly in dreams. I have a near relation who says he always dreams that he has a tooth pulled out before the death of any one of the family or of an intimate friend.

I had a curious dream the other night. I dreamed I was sitting in a little room with a big sheet of paper before me, on which was written in large letters, "On the Philosophy of Life." I was to write an article on the subject. I had absolutely no ideas about the Philosophy of Life, and felt very miserable. Whilst I was pondering over it the door opened, and in came *Slip*. Slip is a small fox terrier, and a particular friend of mine. I cannot say he looks very reputable—he has a sort of rakish appearance about him, and is, in fact, a great rascal, always up to any mischief, with funny ears that flap about when he runs, and small eyes—he always shuts one and winks at you when he feels in safe society. So in came Slip, winking and smiling as dogs can smile, and I asked him immediately for *his* ideas on the subject. I was not at all surprised when he began to speak and answered as follows: "Don't you worry your head about things of that sort. Men are never true philosophers—we dogs know that well. Take your pipe and your cap and let's go for a stroll. It's a glorious evening, and I know a particular spot where there are rabbits. Bother the 'Philosophy of Life.' Tell me rather why rabbits, and rats too, have such confoundedly small holes? Come along, old fellow!" He made some steps towards the door, wagging his little stump of a tail and flapping his funny ears with a knowing look; but all at once he stopped, turned back, came to me, took me by the hand, and winking more than ever, said confidentially in an undertone, "But believe me, my friend, *women* are at the root of all evil."

I awoke, and am still pondering over that dream.

By the way, I heard a touching anecdote about a dog the other day. It is quite true. I knew the dog well—in fact, we were on the most intimate terms. He was a pug, and a very ancient one, and for some time had been in failing health. His constitution was breaking up, but no one imagined that his end was so near. This dog had a wife, but she lived at a house some little distance from his home. One night the dog became worse—as a matter of fact he was dying. Though he must have felt that his last hour had come, that poor dog dragged himself to the abode of his wife, up a flight of stairs,

> And there by her side
> He lay down and died.

(This poetry is original.) Did you ever hear of a more touching exhibition of domestic affection?

Some of my best friends have been dogs. A dog never bothers nor worries one, nor tells one things for one's good, nor remarks how foolish one was to do so and so, nor says, "You see if you had only taken my advice that would never have happened." And who can enter into all one's moods better than a dog? You want to go out, you feel gay and joyous—doggie is game enough, and frisks and barks around you. You want to sit quietly by the fire and think—doggie will sit quietly by the fire and think too. And when you feel utterly miserable and wish you were dead, who comes and licks your hand and looks up with silent sympathy in his big, honest, loving brown eyes, which say as plainly as eyes can speak, "Never mind, old chap, you always have me, you know. *I* shall never leave you."

Dear faithful old doggie! They say you have only instinct and no soul, and will never go to heaven—more's the pity—but if ever there was a true friend you are one.

> Faäithful an' true—them words be i'
> Scriptur—an faäithful an' true
> Ull be fun' upo' four short legs ten
> Times fur one upo' two.

  . . . .

I remember that I have not said anything about the tennis-court at Duino. It was formerly a riding-school, but the roof has been taken off, and the walls make excellent "fielders." Here we were accustomed to disport ourselves every evening. It was interesting to notice the various *characteristic* (that word will please my collaborator—she says one ought always to notice the characteristic features of everything) styles of play: the "Energetic Lady," with her dress pinned up, a large white hat on her head, and a look of intense determination on her face; the "Photographic Lady" progressing about the court with a series of little jumps and bounds, and expressing her feelings by sundry squeaks and screams; my collaborator "serving" with tremendous vigour, but leaving all the after play to her partner and Destiny; Miss Umslopogaas not playing at all, but looking on sweetly with great success; our host playing brilliantly as long as the ball came obligingly to him, but never running at all (a thing distinctly against his principles);

the "Gentle Lunatic" rushing madly about; the "Seal" in gorgeous apparel, trotting along with bristling moustache, and revenging his failures on the unoffending balls; the ponderous "Fat Boy"

LAWN-TENNIS GROUND

with the ground shaking and trembling beneath his elephantine tread; the "Thin Boy" tying himself into intricate knots; the "Other Boy" posing in various elegant statue-like attitudes; and the two learned men, each with a distinct but equally unsuccessful theory.

Lawn-tennis is very popular in Austria, and quite a fashionable game; whilst (alas!) the glorious

ENTRANCE TO THE VILLAGE OF DUINO

games of cricket and football are almost unknown. No wonder, though; cricket and football must be begun in one's earliest boyhood, and boys here are so overburdened with learning that they have very little time for out-of-door sports. I think the educational system on the Continent is a great mistake. They cram all sorts of knowledge into the heads of the miserable children, never thinking of their bodily development and health. What is the result? Every other child one meets wears spectacles, and the sickly appearance of schoolboys generally is something depressing.

> All work and no play
> Makes Jack a dull boy.

Make a note of this, all ye professors and schoolmasters! The moral side, too, is, as a rule, not enough thought of. Surely to teach a boy to fear God, honour the King, Queen, Emperor, or whatever the ruling power is, to be a gentleman, and speak the truth, are, after all, more important factors in his education than all the languages and sciences under the sun.

There! I have preached my little sermon, so will finish the chapter. There is not much in it about "Nothing at all." It would be rather an interesting subject. I will write about it some other time.

CONCLUSION

> What . . .
> I did not well I meant well.
> SHAKESPEARE (*The Winter's Tale*).

AND now these sketches are finished, and there is nothing left but to take farewell. It is always painful to say good-bye, whether to friends or places.

Life is a curious drama, and the scenes change very quickly. Accident, destiny, fate (call it what you like) sends us to some place; we stay there a few days, or weeks, or years; we make friends, we are on the most intimate terms with them; something calls us away; we never return to the well-known spot, and the friends there pass out of our lives—place and friends alike are but a memory.

Memories! how they crowd in on us, and how each year adds to their number! Look back down the fading river of years, and see how they stand out — monuments of bygone days — till they are finally lost in the sea of forgetfulness. Thank God, the pleasant ones last the longest! It seems as if old Time loves to wipe out the painful recollections, and to keep the pleasant ones ever fresh and green.

.   .   .   .   .

I am writing in a railway carriage. The "Gentle Lunatic" is snoring sweetly on the seat opposite me, and the train is taking us every minute farther and farther from Duino.

Good-bye, old castle! May your old walls withstand the wear and tear of many another century. They have been very happy days that I have spent in them, but they are all over. Only in dreams shall I behold your old battlements and towers, the sea in all its blueness breaking at your feet, the sun setting in a sky of golden glory and gilding your gray stones with its dying rays.

Good-bye to all the friends who have made up our party! If ever these sketches should be printed, and you should read them, I hope you will none of you be offended at anything I have written. In case you should be so, I apologise most humbly beforehand, and trust you will forgive me.

Conclusion

And to you, my collaborator, I must also say good-bye for the present.

To you I dedicate these little sketches. If they bring back to you one pleasant thought of the days in Duino,

> Where the world is quiet,

they will have fulfilled their mission.

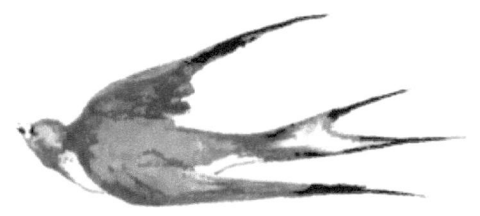

www.ingramcontent.com/pod-product-compliance
Lightning Source LLC
Chambersburg PA
CBHW030336170426
43202CB00010B/1148